C-2246 CAREER EXAMINATION SERIES

This is your
PASSBOOK for...

Public Health Epidemiologist

Test Preparation Study Guide
Questions & Answers

COPYRIGHT NOTICE

This book is SOLELY intended for, is sold ONLY to, and its use is RESTRICTED to individual, bona fide applicants or candidates who qualify by virtue of having seriously filed applications for appropriate license, certificate, professional and/or promotional advancement, higher school matriculation, scholarship, or other legitimate requirements of education and/or governmental authorities.

This book is NOT intended for use, class instruction, tutoring, training, duplication, copying, reprinting, excerption, or adaptation, etc., by:

1) Other publishers
2) Proprietors and/or Instructors of "Coaching" and/or Preparatory Courses
3) Personnel and/or Training Divisions of commercial, industrial, and governmental organizations
4) Schools, colleges, or universities and/or their departments and staffs, including teachers and other personnel
5) Testing Agencies or Bureaus
6) Study groups which seek by the purchase of a single volume to copy and/or duplicate and/or adapt this material for use by the group as a whole without having purchased individual volumes for each of the members of the group
7) Et al.

Such persons would be in violation of appropriate Federal and State statutes.

PROVISION OF LICENSING AGREEMENTS – Recognized educational, commercial, industrial, and governmental institutions and organizations, and others legitimately engaged in educational pursuits, including training, testing, and measurement activities, may address request for a licensing agreement to the copyright owners, who will determine whether, and under what conditions, including fees and charges, the materials in this book may be used them. In other words, a licensing facility exists for the legitimate use of the material in this book on other than an individual basis. However, it is asseverated and affirmed here that the material in this book CANNOT be used without the receipt of the express permission of such a licensing agreement from the Publishers. Inquiries re licensing should be addressed to the company, attention rights and permissions department.

All rights reserved, including the right of reproduction in whole or in part, in any form or by any means, electronic or mechanical, including photocopying, recording, or by any information storage and retrieval system, without permission in writing from the Publisher.

Copyright © 2025 by
National Learning Corporation

212 Michael Drive, Syosset, NY 11791
(516) 921-8888 • www.passbooks.com
E-mail: info@passbooks.com

PASSBOOK® SERIES

THE *PASSBOOK® SERIES* has been created to prepare applicants and candidates for the ultimate academic battlefield – the examination room.

At some time in our lives, each and every one of us may be required to take an examination – for validation, matriculation, admission, qualification, registration, certification, or licensure.

Based on the assumption that every applicant or candidate has met the basic formal educational standards, has taken the required number of courses, and read the necessary texts, the *PASSBOOK® SERIES* furnishes the one special preparation which may assure passing with confidence, instead of failing with insecurity. Examination questions – together with answers – are furnished as the basic vehicle for study so that the mysteries of the examination and its compounding difficulties may be eliminated or diminished by a sure method.

This book is meant to help you pass your examination provided that you qualify and are serious in your objective.

The entire field is reviewed through the huge store of content information which is succinctly presented through a provocative and challenging approach – the question-and-answer method.

A climate of success is established by furnishing the correct answers at the end of each test.

You soon learn to recognize types of questions, forms of questions, and patterns of questioning. You may even begin to anticipate expected outcomes.

You perceive that many questions are repeated or adapted so that you can gain acute insights, which may enable you to score many sure points.

You learn how to confront new questions, or types of questions, and to attack them confidently and work out the correct answers.

You note objectives and emphases, and recognize pitfalls and dangers, so that you may make positive educational adjustments.

Moreover, you are kept fully informed in relation to new concepts, methods, practices, and directions in the field.

You discover that you are actually taking the examination all the time: you are preparing for the examination by "taking" an examination, not by reading extraneous and/or supererogatory textbooks.

In short, this PASSBOOK®, used directedly, should be an important factor in helping you to pass your test.

PUBLIC HEALTH EPIDEMIOLOGIST

DUTIES AND RESPONSIBILITIES
Under general supervision conducts programs for the detection, investigation and prevention of outbreaks of infectious diseases in medical institutions and in the community as a whole; performs related work.

EXAMPLES OF TYPICAL TASKS
Reviews reports of outbreaks of communicable diseases with chiefs of epidemiology; supervises and participates in epidemiological investigations to determine sources of infection or vehicles of transmission; institutes immediate control and preventive measures, such as isolation of cases and immunization and quarantine of contacts in outbreaks of diseases; coordinates outbreak control measures with local health officials and hospital infection committees and epidemiologists; provides information regarding the incidence, control and prevention of infectious diseases to medical practitioners and the general public; assists hospitals in the investigation and control of nosocomial infections; participates in the education of persons in the prevention of specific diseases; participates in field practice programs for nursing and medical students; makes recommendations in epidemiological matters to all other professional disciplines and the community; may conduct studies and investigations in connection with public health problems involving noncommunicable diseases and conditions.

TESTS
The written test may include questions concerning the incidence, control and prevention of infectious diseases, including identification, location and frequency of occurrence, reservoir and vector, mode of transmission, period of communication, susceptibility and resistance to agent; methods of control including preventive measures, control of contacts, immunizations, environmental and epidemiological control measures; medical terminology; medical techniques related to the diagnosis and treatment of infectious diseases; basics of biostatistics; descriptive and quantitative epidemiology; case control, cohort, longitudinal and retrospective studies; odds ratios; active and passive surveillance; modes of disease transmission; epidemiological terminology; and other related areas, including analytical thinking, quantitative analysis & interpretation, adaptability/flexibility, stress tolerance, written comprehension, concern for others, teamwork, integrity, dependability, achievement/effort, attention to detail and self control.

HOW TO TAKE A TEST

I. YOU MUST PASS AN EXAMINATION

A. WHAT EVERY CANDIDATE SHOULD KNOW

Examination applicants often ask us for help in preparing for the written test. What can I study in advance? What kinds of questions will be asked? How will the test be given? How will the papers be graded?

As an applicant for a civil service examination, you may be wondering about some of these things. Our purpose here is to suggest effective methods of advance study and to describe civil service examinations.

Your chances for success on this examination can be increased if you know how to prepare. Those "pre-examination jitters" can be reduced if you know what to expect. You can even experience an adventure in good citizenship if you know why civil service exams are given.

B. WHY ARE CIVIL SERVICE EXAMINATIONS GIVEN?

Civil service examinations are important to you in two ways. As a citizen, you want public jobs filled by employees who know how to do their work. As a job seeker, you want a fair chance to compete for that job on an equal footing with other candidates. The best-known means of accomplishing this two-fold goal is the competitive examination.

Exams are widely publicized throughout the nation. They may be administered for jobs in federal, state, city, municipal, town or village governments or agencies.

Any citizen may apply, with some limitations, such as the age or residence of applicants. Your experience and education may be reviewed to see whether you meet the requirements for the particular examination. When these requirements exist, they are reasonable and applied consistently to all applicants. Thus, a competitive examination may cause you some uneasiness now, but it is your privilege and safeguard.

C. HOW ARE CIVIL SERVICE EXAMS DEVELOPED?

Examinations are carefully written by trained technicians who are specialists in the field known as "psychological measurement," in consultation with recognized authorities in the field of work that the test will cover. These experts recommend the subject matter areas or skills to be tested; only those knowledges or skills important to your success on the job are included. The most reliable books and source materials available are used as references. Together, the experts and technicians judge the difficulty level of the questions.

Test technicians know how to phrase questions so that the problem is clearly stated. Their ethics do not permit "trick" or "catch" questions. Questions may have been tried out on sample groups, or subjected to statistical analysis, to determine their usefulness.

Written tests are often used in combination with performance tests, ratings of training and experience, and oral interviews. All of these measures combine to form the best-known means of finding the right person for the right job.

II. HOW TO PASS THE WRITTEN TEST

A. NATURE OF THE EXAMINATION

To prepare intelligently for civil service examinations, you should know how they differ from school examinations you have taken. In school you were assigned certain definite pages to read or subjects to cover. The examination questions were quite detailed and usually emphasized memory. Civil service exams, on the other hand, try to discover your present ability to perform the duties of a position, plus your potentiality to learn these duties. In other words, a civil service exam attempts to predict how successful you will be. Questions cover such a broad area that they cannot be as minute and detailed as school exam questions.

In the public service similar kinds of work, or positions, are grouped together in one "class." This process is known as *position-classification*. All the positions in a class are paid according to the salary range for that class. One class title covers all of these positions, and they are all tested by the same examination.

B. FOUR BASIC STEPS

1) Study the announcement

How, then, can you know what subjects to study? Our best answer is: "Learn as much as possible about the class of positions for which you've applied." The exam will test the knowledge, skills and abilities needed to do the work.

Your most valuable source of information about the position you want is the official exam announcement. This announcement lists the training and experience qualifications. Check these standards and apply only if you come reasonably close to meeting them.

The brief description of the position in the examination announcement offers some clues to the subjects which will be tested. Think about the job itself. Review the duties in your mind. Can you perform them, or are there some in which you are rusty? Fill in the blank spots in your preparation.

Many jurisdictions preview the written test in the exam announcement by including a section called "Knowledge and Abilities Required," "Scope of the Examination," or some similar heading. Here you will find out specifically what fields will be tested.

2) Review your own background

Once you learn in general what the position is all about, and what you need to know to do the work, ask yourself which subjects you already know fairly well and which need improvement. You may wonder whether to concentrate on improving your strong areas or on building some background in your fields of weakness. When the announcement has specified "some knowledge" or "considerable knowledge," or has used adjectives like "beginning principles of..." or "advanced ... methods," you can get a clue as to the number and difficulty of questions to be asked in any given field. More questions, and hence broader coverage, would be included for those subjects which are more important in the work. Now weigh your strengths and weaknesses against the job requirements and prepare accordingly.

3) Determine the level of the position

Another way to tell how intensively you should prepare is to understand the level of the job for which you are applying. Is it the entering level? In other words, is this the position in which beginners in a field of work are hired? Or is it an intermediate or advanced level? Sometimes this is indicated by such words as "Junior" or "Senior" in the class title. Other jurisdictions use Roman numerals to designate the level – Clerk I, Clerk II, for example. The word "Supervisor" sometimes appears in the title. If the level is not indicated by the title, check the description of duties. Will you be working under very close supervision, or will you have responsibility for independent decisions in this work?

4) Choose appropriate study materials

Now that you know the subjects to be examined and the relative amount of each subject to be covered, you can choose suitable study materials. For beginning level jobs, or even advanced ones, if you have a pronounced weakness in some aspect of your training, read a modern, standard textbook in that field. Be sure it is up to date and has general coverage. Such books are normally available at your library, and the librarian will be glad to help you locate one. For entry-level positions, questions of appropriate difficulty are chosen – neither highly advanced questions, nor those too simple. Such questions require careful thought but not advanced training.

If the position for which you are applying is technical or advanced, you will read more advanced, specialized material. If you are already familiar with the basic principles of your field, elementary textbooks would waste your time. Concentrate on advanced textbooks and technical periodicals. Think through the concepts and review difficult problems in your field.

These are all general sources. You can get more ideas on your own initiative, following these leads. For example, training manuals and publications of the government agency which employs workers in your field can be useful, particularly for technical and professional positions. A letter or visit to the government department involved may result in more specific study suggestions, and certainly will provide you with a more definite idea of the exact nature of the position you are seeking.

III. KINDS OF TESTS

Tests are used for purposes other than measuring knowledge and ability to perform specified duties. For some positions, it is equally important to test ability to make adjustments to new situations or to profit from training. In others, basic mental abilities not dependent on information are essential. Questions which test these things may not appear as pertinent to the duties of the position as those which test for knowledge and information. Yet they are often highly important parts of a fair examination. For very general questions, it is almost impossible to help you direct your study efforts. What we can do is to point out some of the more common of these general abilities needed in public service positions and describe some typical questions.

1) General information

Broad, general information has been found useful for predicting job success in some kinds of work. This is tested in a variety of ways, from vocabulary lists to questions about current events. Basic background in some field of work, such as sociology or economics, may be sampled in a group of questions. Often these are principles which have become familiar to most persons through exposure rather than through formal training. It is difficult to advise you how to study for these questions; being alert to the world around you is our best suggestion.

2) Verbal ability

An example of an ability needed in many positions is verbal or language ability. Verbal ability is, in brief, the ability to use and understand words. Vocabulary and grammar tests are typical measures of this ability. Reading comprehension or paragraph interpretation questions are common in many kinds of civil service tests. You are given a paragraph of written material and asked to find its central meaning.

3) Numerical ability

Number skills can be tested by the familiar arithmetic problem, by checking paired lists of numbers to see which are alike and which are different, or by interpreting charts and graphs. In the latter test, a graph may be printed in the test booklet which you are asked to use as the basis for answering questions.

4) Observation

A popular test for law-enforcement positions is the observation test. A picture is shown to you for several minutes, then taken away. Questions about the picture test your ability to observe both details and larger elements.

5) Following directions

In many positions in the public service, the employee must be able to carry out written instructions dependably and accurately. You may be given a chart with several columns, each column listing a variety of information. The questions require you to carry out directions involving the information given in the chart.

6) Skills and aptitudes

Performance tests effectively measure some manual skills and aptitudes. When the skill is one in which you are trained, such as typing or shorthand, you can practice. These tests are often very much like those given in business school or high school courses. For many of the other skills and aptitudes, however, no short-time preparation can be made. Skills and abilities natural to you or that you have developed throughout your lifetime are being tested.

Many of the general questions just described provide all the data needed to answer the questions and ask you to use your reasoning ability to find the answers. Your best preparation for these tests, as well as for tests of facts and ideas, is to be at your physical and mental best. You, no doubt, have your own methods of getting into an exam-taking mood and keeping "in shape." The next section lists some ideas on this subject.

IV. KINDS OF QUESTIONS

Only rarely is the "essay" question, which you answer in narrative form, used in civil service tests. Civil service tests are usually of the short-answer type. Full instructions for answering these questions will be given to you at the examination. But in case this is your first experience with short-answer questions and separate answer sheets, here is what you need to know:

1) **Multiple-choice Questions**

Most popular of the short-answer questions is the "multiple choice" or "best answer" question. It can be used, for example, to test for factual knowledge, ability to solve problems or judgment in meeting situations found at work.

A multiple-choice question is normally one of three types—
- It can begin with an incomplete statement followed by several possible endings. You are to find the one ending which *best* completes the statement, although some of the others may not be entirely wrong.
- It can also be a complete statement in the form of a question which is answered by choosing one of the statements listed.

- It can be in the form of a problem – again you select the best answer.

Here is an example of a multiple-choice question with a discussion which should give you some clues as to the method for choosing the right answer:

When an employee has a complaint about his assignment, the action which will *best* help him overcome his difficulty is to
  A. discuss his difficulty with his coworkers
  B. take the problem to the head of the organization
  C. take the problem to the person who gave him the assignment
  D. say nothing to anyone about his complaint

In answering this question, you should study each of the choices to find which is best. Consider choice "A" – Certainly an employee may discuss his complaint with fellow employees, but no change or improvement can result, and the complaint remains unresolved. Choice "B" is a poor choice since the head of the organization probably does not know what assignment you have been given, and taking your problem to him is known as "going over the head" of the supervisor. The supervisor, or person who made the assignment, is the person who can clarify it or correct any injustice. Choice "C" is, therefore, correct. To say nothing, as in choice "D," is unwise. Supervisors have and interest in knowing the problems employees are facing, and the employee is seeking a solution to his problem.

2) True/False Questions

The "true/false" or "right/wrong" form of question is sometimes used. Here a complete statement is given. Your job is to decide whether the statement is right or wrong.

SAMPLE: A roaming cell-phone call to a nearby city costs less than a non-roaming call to a distant city.

This statement is wrong, or false, since roaming calls are more expensive.

This is not a complete list of all possible question forms, although most of the others are variations of these common types. You will always get complete directions for answering questions. Be sure you understand *how* to mark your answers – ask questions until you do.

V. RECORDING YOUR ANSWERS

Computer terminals are used more and more today for many different kinds of exams.
For an examination with very few applicants, you may be told to record your answers in the test booklet itself. Separate answer sheets are much more common. If this separate answer sheet is to be scored by machine – and this is often the case – it is highly important that you mark your answers correctly in order to get credit.

An electronic scoring machine is often used in civil service offices because of the speed with which papers can be scored. Machine-scored answer sheets must be marked with a pencil, which will be given to you. This pencil has a high graphite content which responds to the electronic scoring machine. As a matter of fact, stray dots may register as answers, so do not let your pencil rest on the answer sheet while you are pondering the correct answer. Also, if your pencil lead breaks or is otherwise defective, ask for another.

Since the answer sheet will be dropped in a slot in the scoring machine, be careful not to bend the corners or get the paper crumpled.

The answer sheet normally has five vertical columns of numbers, with 30 numbers to a column. These numbers correspond to the question numbers in your test booklet. After each number, going across the page are four or five pairs of dotted lines. These short dotted lines have small letters or numbers above them. The first two pairs may also have a "T" or "F" above the letters. This indicates that the first two pairs only are to be used if the questions are of the true-false type. If the questions are multiple choice, disregard the "T" and "F" and pay attention only to the small letters or numbers.

Answer your questions in the manner of the sample that follows:

32. The largest city in the United States is
    A. Washington, D.C.
    B. New York City
    C. Chicago
    D. Detroit
    E. San Francisco

1) Choose the answer you think is best. (New York City is the largest, so "B" is correct.)
2) Find the row of dotted lines numbered the same as the question you are answering. (Find row number 32)
3) Find the pair of dotted lines corresponding to the answer. (Find the pair of lines under the mark "B.")
4) Make a solid black mark between the dotted lines.

VI. BEFORE THE TEST

Common sense will help you find procedures to follow to get ready for an examination. Too many of us, however, overlook these sensible measures. Indeed, nervousness and fatigue have been found to be the most serious reasons why applicants fail to do their best on civil service tests. Here is a list of reminders:

- Begin your preparation early – Don't wait until the last minute to go scurrying around for books and materials or to find out what the position is all about.
- Prepare continuously – An hour a night for a week is better than an all-night cram session. This has been definitely established. What is more, a night a week for a month will return better dividends than crowding your study into a shorter period of time.
- Locate the place of the exam – You have been sent a notice telling you when and where to report for the examination. If the location is in a different town or otherwise unfamiliar to you, it would be well to inquire the best route and learn something about the building.
- Relax the night before the test – Allow your mind to rest. Do not study at all that night. Plan some mild recreation or diversion; then go to bed early and get a good night's sleep.
- Get up early enough to make a leisurely trip to the place for the test – This way unforeseen events, traffic snarls, unfamiliar buildings, etc. will not upset you.
- Dress comfortably – A written test is not a fashion show. You will be known by number and not by name, so wear something comfortable.

- Leave excess paraphernalia at home – Shopping bags and odd bundles will get in your way. You need bring only the items mentioned in the official notice you received; usually everything you need is provided. Do not bring reference books to the exam. They will only confuse those last minutes and be taken away from you when in the test room.
- Arrive somewhat ahead of time – If because of transportation schedules you must get there very early, bring a newspaper or magazine to take your mind off yourself while waiting.
- Locate the examination room – When you have found the proper room, you will be directed to the seat or part of the room where you will sit. Sometimes you are given a sheet of instructions to read while you are waiting. Do not fill out any forms until you are told to do so; just read them and be prepared.
- Relax and prepare to listen to the instructions
- If you have any physical problem that may keep you from doing your best, be sure to tell the test administrator. If you are sick or in poor health, you really cannot do your best on the exam. You can come back and take the test some other time.

VII. AT THE TEST

The day of the test is here and you have the test booklet in your hand. The temptation to get going is very strong. Caution! There is more to success than knowing the right answers. You must know how to identify your papers and understand variations in the type of short-answer question used in this particular examination. Follow these suggestions for maximum results from your efforts:

1) Cooperate with the monitor

The test administrator has a duty to create a situation in which you can be as much at ease as possible. He will give instructions, tell you when to begin, check to see that you are marking your answer sheet correctly, and so on. He is not there to guard you, although he will see that your competitors do not take unfair advantage. He wants to help you do your best.

2) Listen to all instructions

Don't jump the gun! Wait until you understand all directions. In most civil service tests you get more time than you need to answer the questions. So don't be in a hurry. Read each word of instructions until you clearly understand the meaning. Study the examples, listen to all announcements and follow directions. Ask questions if you do not understand what to do.

3) Identify your papers

Civil service exams are usually identified by number only. You will be assigned a number; you must not put your name on your test papers. Be sure to copy your number correctly. Since more than one exam may be given, copy your exact examination title.

4) Plan your time

Unless you are told that a test is a "speed" or "rate of work" test, speed itself is usually not important. Time enough to answer all the questions will be provided, but this does not mean that you have all day. An overall time limit has been set. Divide the total time (in minutes) by the number of questions to determine the approximate time you have for each question.

5) Do not linger over difficult questions

If you come across a difficult question, mark it with a paper clip (useful to have along) and come back to it when you have been through the booklet. One caution if you do this – be sure to skip a number on your answer sheet as well. Check often to be sure that you have not lost your place and that you are marking in the row numbered the same as the question you are answering.

6) Read the questions

Be sure you know what the question asks! Many capable people are unsuccessful because they failed to *read* the questions correctly.

7) Answer all questions

Unless you have been instructed that a penalty will be deducted for incorrect answers, it is better to guess than to omit a question.

8) Speed tests

It is often better NOT to guess on speed tests. It has been found that on timed tests people are tempted to spend the last few seconds before time is called in marking answers at random – without even reading them – in the hope of picking up a few extra points. To discourage this practice, the instructions may warn you that your score will be "corrected" for guessing. That is, a penalty will be applied. The incorrect answers will be deducted from the correct ones, or some other penalty formula will be used.

9) Review your answers

If you finish before time is called, go back to the questions you guessed or omitted to give them further thought. Review other answers if you have time.

10) Return your test materials

If you are ready to leave before others have finished or time is called, take ALL your materials to the monitor and leave quietly. Never take any test material with you. The monitor can discover whose papers are not complete, and taking a test booklet may be grounds for disqualification.

VIII. EXAMINATION TECHNIQUES

1) Read the general instructions carefully. These are usually printed on the first page of the exam booklet. As a rule, these instructions refer to the timing of the examination; the fact that you should not start work until the signal and must stop work at a signal, etc. If there are any *special* instructions, such as a choice of questions to be answered, make sure that you note this instruction carefully.

2) When you are ready to start work on the examination, that is as soon as the signal has been given, read the instructions to each question booklet, underline any key words or phrases, such as *least, best, outline, describe* and the like. In this way you will tend to answer as requested rather than discover on reviewing your paper that you *listed without describing*, that you selected the *worst* choice rather than the *best* choice, etc.

3) If the examination is of the objective or multiple-choice type – that is, each question will also give a series of possible answers: A, B, C or D, and you are called upon to select the best answer and write the letter next to that answer on your answer paper – it is advisable to start answering each question in turn. There may be anywhere from 50 to 100 such questions in the three or four hours allotted and you can see how much time would be taken if you read through all the questions before beginning to answer any. Furthermore, if you come across a question or group of questions which you know would be difficult to answer, it would undoubtedly affect your handling of all the other questions.

4) If the examination is of the essay type and contains but a few questions, it is a moot point as to whether you should read all the questions before starting to answer any one. Of course, if you are given a choice – say five out of seven and the like – then it is essential to read all the questions so you can eliminate the two that are most difficult. If, however, you are asked to answer all the questions, there may be danger in trying to answer the easiest one first because you may find that you will spend too much time on it. The best technique is to answer the first question, then proceed to the second, etc.

5) Time your answers. Before the exam begins, write down the time it started, then add the time allowed for the examination and write down the time it must be completed, then divide the time available somewhat as follows:
    - If 3-1/2 hours are allowed, that would be 210 minutes. If you have 80 objective-type questions, that would be an average of 2-1/2 minutes per question. Allow yourself no more than 2 minutes per question, or a total of 160 minutes, which will permit about 50 minutes to review.
    - If for the time allotment of 210 minutes there are 7 essay questions to answer, that would average about 30 minutes a question. Give yourself only 25 minutes per question so that you have about 35 minutes to review.

6) The most important instruction is to *read each question* and make sure you know what is wanted. The second most important instruction is to *time yourself properly* so that you answer every question. The third most important instruction is to *answer every question*. Guess if you have to but include something for each question. Remember that you will receive no credit for a blank and will probably receive some credit if you write something in answer to an essay question. If you guess a letter – say "B" for a multiple-choice question – you may have guessed right. If you leave a blank as an answer to a multiple-choice question, the examiners may respect your feelings but it will not add a point to your score. Some exams may penalize you for wrong answers, so in such cases *only*, you may not want to guess unless you have some basis for your answer.

7) Suggestions
    a. Objective-type questions
        1. Examine the question booklet for proper sequence of pages and questions
        2. Read all instructions carefully
        3. Skip any question which seems too difficult; return to it after all other questions have been answered
        4. Apportion your time properly; do not spend too much time on any single question or group of questions

5. Note and underline key words – *all, most, fewest, least, best, worst, same, opposite,* etc.
6. Pay particular attention to negatives
7. Note unusual option, e.g., unduly long, short, complex, different or similar in content to the body of the question
8. Observe the use of "hedging" words – *probably, may, most likely,* etc.
9. Make sure that your answer is put next to the same number as the question
10. Do not second-guess unless you have good reason to believe the second answer is definitely more correct
11. Cross out original answer if you decide another answer is more accurate; do not erase until you are ready to hand your paper in
12. Answer all questions; guess unless instructed otherwise
13. Leave time for review

b. Essay questions
   1. Read each question carefully
   2. Determine exactly what is wanted. Underline key words or phrases.
   3. Decide on outline or paragraph answer
   4. Include many different points and elements unless asked to develop any one or two points or elements
   5. Show impartiality by giving pros and cons unless directed to select one side only
   6. Make and write down any assumptions you find necessary to answer the questions
   7. Watch your English, grammar, punctuation and choice of words
   8. Time your answers; don't crowd material

8) Answering the essay question

Most essay questions can be answered by framing the specific response around several key words or ideas. Here are a few such key words or ideas:

M's: manpower, materials, methods, money, management
P's: purpose, program, policy, plan, procedure, practice, problems, pitfalls, personnel, public relations
   a. Six basic steps in handling problems:
      1. Preliminary plan and background development
      2. Collect information, data and facts
      3. Analyze and interpret information, data and facts
      4. Analyze and develop solutions as well as make recommendations
      5. Prepare report and sell recommendations
      6. Install recommendations and follow up effectiveness

   b. Pitfalls to avoid
      1. *Taking things for granted* – A statement of the situation does not necessarily imply that each of the elements is necessarily true; for example, a complaint may be invalid and biased so that all that can be taken for granted is that a complaint has been registered

2. *Considering only one side of a situation* – Wherever possible, indicate several alternatives and then point out the reasons you selected the best one
3. *Failing to indicate follow up* – Whenever your answer indicates action on your part, make certain that you will take proper follow-up action to see how successful your recommendations, procedures or actions turn out to be
4. *Taking too long in answering any single question* – Remember to time your answers properly

IX. AFTER THE TEST

Scoring procedures differ in detail among civil service jurisdictions although the general principles are the same. Whether the papers are hand-scored or graded by machine we have described, they are nearly always graded by number. That is, the person who marks the paper knows only the number – never the name – of the applicant. Not until all the papers have been graded will they be matched with names. If other tests, such as training and experience or oral interview ratings have been given, scores will be combined. Different parts of the examination usually have different weights. For example, the written test might count 60 percent of the final grade, and a rating of training and experience 40 percent. In many jurisdictions, veterans will have a certain number of points added to their grades.

After the final grade has been determined, the names are placed in grade order and an eligible list is established. There are various methods for resolving ties between those who get the same final grade – probably the most common is to place first the name of the person whose application was received first. Job offers are made from the eligible list in the order the names appear on it. You will be notified of your grade and your rank as soon as all these computations have been made. This will be done as rapidly as possible.

People who are found to meet the requirements in the announcement are called "eligibles." Their names are put on a list of eligible candidates. An eligible's chances of getting a job depend on how high he stands on this list and how fast agencies are filling jobs from the list.

When a job is to be filled from a list of eligibles, the agency asks for the names of people on the list of eligibles for that job. When the civil service commission receives this request, it sends to the agency the names of the three people highest on this list. Or, if the job to be filled has specialized requirements, the office sends the agency the names of the top three persons who meet these requirements from the general list.

The appointing officer makes a choice from among the three people whose names were sent to him. If the selected person accepts the appointment, the names of the others are put back on the list to be considered for future openings.

That is the rule in hiring from all kinds of eligible lists, whether they are for typist, carpenter, chemist, or something else. For every vacancy, the appointing officer has his choice of any one of the top three eligibles on the list. This explains why the person whose name is on top of the list sometimes does not get an appointment when some of the persons lower on the list do. If the appointing officer chooses the second or third eligible, the No. 1 eligible does not get a job at once, but stays on the list until he is appointed or the list is terminated.

X. HOW TO PASS THE INTERVIEW TEST

The examination for which you applied requires an oral interview test. You have already taken the written test and you are now being called for the interview test – the final part of the formal examination.

You may think that it is not possible to prepare for an interview test and that there are no procedures to follow during an interview. Our purpose is to point out some things you can do in advance that will help you and some good rules to follow and pitfalls to avoid while you are being interviewed.

What is an interview supposed to test?

The written examination is designed to test the technical knowledge and competence of the candidate; the oral is designed to evaluate intangible qualities, not readily measured otherwise, and to establish a list showing the relative fitness of each candidate – as measured against his competitors – for the position sought. Scoring is not on the basis of "right" and "wrong," but on a sliding scale of values ranging from "not passable" to "outstanding." As a matter of fact, it is possible to achieve a relatively low score without a single "incorrect" answer because of evident weakness in the qualities being measured.

Occasionally, an examination may consist entirely of an oral test – either an individual or a group oral. In such cases, information is sought concerning the technical knowledges and abilities of the candidate, since there has been no written examination for this purpose. More commonly, however, an oral test is used to supplement a written examination.

Who conducts interviews?

The composition of oral boards varies among different jurisdictions. In nearly all, a representative of the personnel department serves as chairman. One of the members of the board may be a representative of the department in which the candidate would work. In some cases, "outside experts" are used, and, frequently, a businessman or some other representative of the general public is asked to serve. Labor and management or other special groups may be represented. The aim is to secure the services of experts in the appropriate field.

However the board is composed, it is a good idea (and not at all improper or unethical) to ascertain in advance of the interview who the members are and what groups they represent. When you are introduced to them, you will have some idea of their backgrounds and interests, and at least you will not stutter and stammer over their names.

What should be done before the interview?

While knowledge about the board members is useful and takes some of the surprise element out of the interview, there is other preparation which is more substantive. It *is* possible to prepare for an oral interview – in several ways:

1) Keep a copy of your application and review it carefully before the interview

This may be the only document before the oral board, and the starting point of the interview. Know what education and experience you have listed there, and the sequence and dates of all of it. Sometimes the board will ask you to review the highlights of your experience for them; you should not have to hem and haw doing it.

2) Study the class specification and the examination announcement

Usually, the oral board has one or both of these to guide them. The qualities, characteristics or knowledges required by the position sought are stated in these documents. They offer valuable clues as to the nature of the oral interview. For example, if the job involves supervisory responsibilities, the announcement will usually indicate that knowledge of modern supervisory methods and the qualifications of the candidate as a supervisor will be tested. If so, you can expect such questions, frequently in the form of a hypothetical situation which you are expected to solve. NEVER go into an oral without knowledge of the duties and responsibilities of the job you seek.

3) Think through each qualification required

Try to visualize the kind of questions you would ask if you were a board member. How well could you answer them? Try especially to appraise your own knowledge and background in each area, *measured against the job sought*, and identify any areas in which you are weak. Be critical and realistic – do not flatter yourself.

4) Do some general reading in areas in which you feel you may be weak

For example, if the job involves supervision and your past experience has NOT, some general reading in supervisory methods and practices, particularly in the field of human relations, might be useful. Do NOT study agency procedures or detailed manuals. The oral board will be testing your understanding and capacity, not your memory.

5) Get a good night's sleep and watch your general health and mental attitude

You will want a clear head at the interview. Take care of a cold or any other minor ailment, and of course, no hangovers.

What should be done on the day of the interview?

Now comes the day of the interview itself. Give yourself plenty of time to get there. Plan to arrive somewhat ahead of the scheduled time, particularly if your appointment is in the fore part of the day. If a previous candidate fails to appear, the board might be ready for you a bit early. By early afternoon an oral board is almost invariably behind schedule if there are many candidates, and you may have to wait. Take along a book or magazine to read, or your application to review, but leave any extraneous material in the waiting room when you go in for your interview. In any event, relax and compose yourself.

The matter of dress is important. The board is forming impressions about you – from your experience, your manners, your attitude, and your appearance. Give your personal appearance careful attention. Dress your best, but not your flashiest. Choose conservative, appropriate clothing, and be sure it is immaculate. This is a business interview, and your appearance should indicate that you regard it as such. Besides, being well groomed and properly dressed will help boost your confidence.

Sooner or later, someone will call your name and escort you into the interview room. *This is it.* From here on you are on your own. It is too late for any more preparation. But remember, you asked for this opportunity to prove your fitness, and you are here because your request was granted.

What happens when you go in?

The usual sequence of events will be as follows: The clerk (who is often the board stenographer) will introduce you to the chairman of the oral board, who will introduce you to the other members of the board. Acknowledge the introductions before you sit down. Do not be surprised if you find a microphone facing you or a stenotypist sitting by. Oral interviews are usually recorded in the event of an appeal or other review.

Usually the chairman of the board will open the interview by reviewing the highlights of your education and work experience from your application – primarily for the benefit of the other members of the board, as well as to get the material into the record. Do not interrupt or comment unless there is an error or significant misinterpretation; if that is the case, do not hesitate. But do not quibble about insignificant matters. Also, he will usually ask you some question about your education, experience or your present job – partly to get you to start talking and to establish the interviewing "rapport." He may start the actual questioning, or turn it over to one of the other members. Frequently, each member undertakes the questioning on a particular area, one in which he is perhaps most competent, so you can expect each member to participate in the examination. Because time is limited, you may also expect some rather abrupt switches in the direction the questioning takes, so do not be upset by it. Normally, a board member will not pursue a single line of questioning unless he discovers a particular strength or weakness.

After each member has participated, the chairman will usually ask whether any member has any further questions, then will ask you if you have anything you wish to add. Unless you are expecting this question, it may floor you. Worse, it may start you off on an extended, extemporaneous speech. The board is not usually seeking more information. The question is principally to offer you a last opportunity to present further qualifications or to indicate that you have nothing to add. So, if you feel that a significant qualification or characteristic has been overlooked, it is proper to point it out in a sentence or so. Do not compliment the board on the thoroughness of their examination – they have been sketchy, and you know it. If you wish, merely say, "No thank you, I have nothing further to add." This is a point where you can "talk yourself out" of a good impression or fail to present an important bit of information. Remember, *you close the interview yourself*.

The chairman will then say, "That is all, Mr. _____, thank you." Do not be startled; the interview is over, and quicker than you think. Thank him, gather your belongings and take your leave. Save your sigh of relief for the other side of the door.

How to put your best foot forward

Throughout this entire process, you may feel that the board individually and collectively is trying to pierce your defenses, seek out your hidden weaknesses and embarrass and confuse you. Actually, this is not true. They are obliged to make an appraisal of your qualifications for the job you are seeking, and they want to see you in your best light. Remember, they must interview all candidates and a non-cooperative candidate may become a failure in spite of their best efforts to bring out his qualifications. Here are 15 suggestions that will help you:

1) Be natural – Keep your attitude confident, not cocky

If you are not confident that you can do the job, do not expect the board to be. Do not apologize for your weaknesses, try to bring out your strong points. The board is interested in a positive, not negative, presentation. Cockiness will antagonize any board member and make him wonder if you are covering up a weakness by a false show of strength.

2) Get comfortable, but don't lounge or sprawl

Sit erectly but not stiffly. A careless posture may lead the board to conclude that you are careless in other things, or at least that you are not impressed by the importance of the occasion. Either conclusion is natural, even if incorrect. Do not fuss with your clothing, a pencil or an ashtray. Your hands may occasionally be useful to emphasize a point; do not let them become a point of distraction.

3) Do not wisecrack or make small talk

This is a serious situation, and your attitude should show that you consider it as such. Further, the time of the board is limited – they do not want to waste it, and neither should you.

4) Do not exaggerate your experience or abilities
In the first place, from information in the application or other interviews and sources, the board may know more about you than you think. Secondly, you probably will not get away with it. An experienced board is rather adept at spotting such a situation, so do not take the chance.

5) If you know a board member, do not make a point of it, yet do not hide it
Certainly you are not fooling him, and probably not the other members of the board. Do not try to take advantage of your acquaintanceship – it will probably do you little good.

6) Do not dominate the interview
Let the board do that. They will give you the clues – do not assume that you have to do all the talking. Realize that the board has a number of questions to ask you, and do not try to take up all the interview time by showing off your extensive knowledge of the answer to the first one.

7) Be attentive
You only have 20 minutes or so, and you should keep your attention at its sharpest throughout. When a member is addressing a problem or question to you, give him your undivided attention. Address your reply principally to him, but do not exclude the other board members.

8) Do not interrupt
A board member may be stating a problem for you to analyze. He will ask you a question when the time comes. Let him state the problem, and wait for the question.

9) Make sure you understand the question
Do not try to answer until you are sure what the question is. If it is not clear, restate it in your own words or ask the board member to clarify it for you. However, do not haggle about minor elements.

10) Reply promptly but not hastily
A common entry on oral board rating sheets is "candidate responded readily," or "candidate hesitated in replies." Respond as promptly and quickly as you can, but do not jump to a hasty, ill-considered answer.

11) Do not be peremptory in your answers
A brief answer is proper – but do not fire your answer back. That is a losing game from your point of view. The board member can probably ask questions much faster than you can answer them.

12) Do not try to create the answer you think the board member wants
He is interested in what kind of mind you have and how it works – not in playing games. Furthermore, he can usually spot this practice and will actually grade you down on it.

13) Do not switch sides in your reply merely to agree with a board member
Frequently, a member will take a contrary position merely to draw you out and to see if you are willing and able to defend your point of view. Do not start a debate, yet do not surrender a good position. If a position is worth taking, it is worth defending.

14) Do not be afraid to admit an error in judgment if you are shown to be wrong

The board knows that you are forced to reply without any opportunity for careful consideration. Your answer may be demonstrably wrong. If so, admit it and get on with the interview.

15) Do not dwell at length on your present job

The opening question may relate to your present assignment. Answer the question but do not go into an extended discussion. You are being examined for a *new* job, not your present one. As a matter of fact, try to phrase ALL your answers in terms of the job for which you are being examined.

Basis of Rating

Probably you will forget most of these "do's" and "don'ts" when you walk into the oral interview room. Even remembering them all will not ensure you a passing grade. Perhaps you did not have the qualifications in the first place. But remembering them will help you to put your best foot forward, without treading on the toes of the board members.

Rumor and popular opinion to the contrary notwithstanding, an oral board wants you to make the best appearance possible. They know you are under pressure – but they also want to see how you respond to it as a guide to what your reaction would be under the pressures of the job you seek. They will be influenced by the degree of poise you display, the personal traits you show and the manner in which you respond.

ABOUT THIS BOOK

This book contains tests divided into Examination Sections. Go through each test, answering every question in the margin. We have also attached a sample answer sheet at the back of the book that can be removed and used. At the end of each test look at the answer key and check your answers. On the ones you got wrong, look at the right answer choice and learn. Do not fill in the answers first. Do not memorize the questions and answers, but understand the answer and principles involved. On your test, the questions will likely be different from the samples. Questions are changed and new ones added. If you understand these past questions you should have success with any changes that arise. Tests may consist of several types of questions. We have additional books on each subject should more study be advisable or necessary for you. Finally, the more you study, the better prepared you will be. This book is intended to be the last thing you study before you walk into the examination room. Prior study of relevant texts is also recommended. NLC publishes some of these in our Fundamental Series. Knowledge and good sense are important factors in passing your exam. Good luck also helps. So now study this Passbook, absorb the material contained within and take that knowledge into the examination. Then do your best to pass that exam.

EXAMINATION SECTION

EXAMINATION SECTION
TEST 1

DIRECTIONS: Each question or incomplete statement is followed by several suggested answers or completions. Select the one the BEST answers the question or completes the statement. *PRINT THE LETTER OF THE CORRECT ANSWER IN THE SPACE AT THE RIGHT.*

1. A health educator helps collect data for an epidemiological study that will examine the relationship, during the months of December and January, between the incidence of influenza in a community and the behaviors of the community members. The type of study to be conducted will be

    A. longitudinal
    B. ex post facto
    C. cross-sectional
    D. pre-test/post-test

    1.____

2. In a worksite wellness program, which of the following is LEAST likely to help employees change their health risks?

    A. The use of "engagement" strategies that are individually designed
    B. A solid and focused array of health improvement classes and seminars
    C. Repeated follow-up contacts after programs or classes have ended
    D. Persistent, personalized outreach to at-risk employees

    2.____

3. The final phase of the PRECEDE model of planning health education is the _____ diagnosis.

    A. behavioral
    B. administrative
    C. educational
    D. social

    3.____

4. Typically, a health promotion effort in a community should begin with a(n)

    A. enhancement of community awareness about the program
    B. behavioral change strategy
    C. screening and appraisal of health risks
    D. socioemotional intervention

    4.____

5. Role-playing exercises are sometimes a useful means of instruction in health education. Generally, a disadvantage associated with this activity is that it

    A. focuses on a narrow band of skills
    B. tends to truncate discussions
    C. makes learning more abstract
    D. requires a well-trained facilitator

    5.____

6. In researching a community profile, which of the following items of information would probably be LEAST useful to a health educator?

    A. Average educational level of residents
    B. Age distribution

    6.____

C. Political affiliations
D. Average household income

7. A health educator decides that in conducting a course for young teenagers on the dangers of unprotected sex, he will adopt a paternalistic communication style. A potential disadvantage associated with this decision is that

   A. attention is often diverted from real problems
   B. clients may become reluctant to take independent action
   C. clients may become likely to rebel or reject the views of the health educator
   D. the health educator may be perceived as neither supportive nor caring

8. To help conduct effective meetings, health educators and other program members should

   A. begin only when all members of the group are present
   B. record minutes of each meeting and distribute them before the next
   C. take collective responsibility for tasks and deadlines
   D. let people raise issues that are important to them, even if they are not on the agenda

9. Though the cultural groups that make up the broad category known as "Asian American" are varied in their beliefs and customs, it should generally be expected that first-generation immigrants from Asia will share a set of traditional values and behavior. Which of the following would be LEAST likely to be included in these values and behaviors?

   A. Assertive help-seeking in time of need
   B. Blame of self for failure
   C. Control of strong feelings
   D. Respect for authority

10. As a general rule, sentences that appear in a health education brochure should each contain about _____ or fewer words.

    A. 8
    B. 12
    C. 17
    D. 25

11. A health educator is participating in the writing of a grant proposal for a hygiene awareness program for migrant workers. Typically, the body of a proposal should FIRST contain

    A. specific goals and objectives of the program
    B. a description of the target population
    C. an itemized budget for the program, including all expenses and a justification for each
    D. a one-page summary of the entire proposal

12. When defining and organizing a message for an adult audience with limited reading skills, a health educator should NOT

    A. put the most important information in the middle of the presentation
    B. present one idea on a single page, or two facing pages

C. frequently summarize or repeat concepts
D. start with the completed idea one wants understood, then provide a breakdown or explanation

13. Which of the following theories would be MOST helpful in designing a program for treating alcohol abuse? 13.____

    A. Consensus
    B. Innovation-diffusion
    C. Conflict
    D. Self-regulation

14. As a mass media channel for the communication of a health-related message or public service announcement, magazines 14.____

    A. are more approachable and involve easier placement of PSAs than audiovisual media
    B. do not enable agencies to more specifically target segments of the public
    C. can explain more complex health issues and behaviors
    D. generally involve passive consumption

15. Which of the following is a risk factor associated with stroke? 15.____

    A. Alcohol abuse
    B. Obesity
    C. Home hazards
    D. Infectious agents

16. Before deciding upon a means of instruction, a health educator should know that people generally retain only about 10 percent of content that they 16.____

    A. say
    B. read
    C. do
    D. hear

17. For participants in a breast and cervical cancer control program, a health educator adapted a low-literacy flier developed by another organization. The flier was pre-tested among community members, and found to be written at the appropriate level. Staff at the agency observed that women in the program, after receiving the fliers, folded them to fit them in their purses, and many women left the fliers behind in the clinic. The most appropriate next step would be to 17.____

    A. conduct a focus group to discover what kind of format women would prefer for written information
    B. modify the format but keep the original text, to produce a flier that will fit into a woman's purse
    C. discontinue production of the fliers, and instead rely on visual presentation of the material on-site
    D. monitor the women as they leave the clinic and encourage them to take the flier with them

18. As part of a community assessment, a health educator wants to conduct a focus group interview. The ideal number of members to participate in this sort of group is usually about

    A. 3 to 5
    B. 4 to 8
    C. 10 to 12
    D. 15 to 20

19. In the client-centered model of health education, interventions are best described as

    A. promotion of medical interventions to prevent or alleviate ill health
    B. instruction about the causes and effects of health-demoting factors
    C. changing clients' attitudes and behaviors to promote the adoption of a healthier lifestyle
    D. collaborations with clients to identify and act on health-related concerns

20. Each of the following is a guideline that should be used in acquiring information from clients who are of different cultural or language backgrounds, EXCEPT

    A. asking questions in the exact same way repeatedly, to ensure understanding
    B. adjusting the style of the interaction to reflect differences in age between oneself and the client
    C. establishing rapport and showing genuine warm concern for the client, to build trust
    D. using open-ended questions to increase the amount of information obtained

21. The local newspaper has just run a story about a homeless encampment near the downtown area of a small city. An educator with the local health agency wants to write a letter to the editor of the paper, in order to draw attention to the services it offers to homeless people in the community. Guidelines for writing letters to be printed on the editorial page include
    I. the most important point should be made at the end of the letter
    II. letters should be saved for the most important issues
    III. letters should be signed by an officer of the organization
    IV. they should be no longer than 50-100 words

    A. I and II
    B. II and III
    C. III and IV
    D. I, II, III and IV

22. The lead agency in a coalition for health education and promotion should usually expect extensive staff demands in each of the following areas, EXCEPT

    A. clerical
    B. service delivery
    C. fund-raising
    D. research and fact gathering

23. A health agency conducts a readability test on one of its brochures. This is a(n) _____ evaluation of a health education procedure.   23.____

    A. impact
    B. process
    C. outcome
    D. formative

24. Most nationwide initiatives focusing on public health, such as Healthy People 2000, place the highest priority on   24.____

    A. physical activity and fitness
    B. family planning
    C. occupational safety and health
    D. violent and abusive behavior

25. A health educator designs a number of goals for his exercise education program, beginning at the individual consciousness level and moving to social change. The educator will have accomplished a decision-making change goal if, after completing the program, a client can say that she   25.____

    A. feels unfit because she gets out of breath easily
    B. will take fitness classes
    C. states the belief that she would feel better if she exercised more
    D. now goes to the gym regularly and is generally more physically active

---

KEY (CORRECT ANSWERS)

1. C	11. D
2. B	12. A
3. B	13. D
4. C	14. C
5. D	15. A
6. C	16. B
7. B	17. B
8. B	18. C
9. A	19. D
10. C	20. A

21. B
22. B
23. D
24. A
25. B

TEST 2

DIRECTIONS: Each question or incomplete statement is followed by several suggested answers or completions. Select the one the BEST answers the question or completes the statement. *PRINT THE LETTER OF THE CORRECT ANSWER IN THE SPACE AT THE RIGHT.*

1. Which of the following is an example of secondary health education?

    A. Demonstrating the proper installation of a child car seat
    B. Explaining to a group of teens how to avoid contracting sexually transmitted diseases such as AIDS
    C. Showing clients how to give first aid after an accident
    D. Teaching a client with food allergies how to adjust eating habits to ensure minimum complications

2. A health educator wants to print a brochure on safe sex to be distributed among local teenagers. The educator should know that the greatest expense involved in printing materials is

    A. making the printing plates
    B. paper
    C. distribution costs
    D. original artwork or graphics

3. In the beginning phase of a health education program, a good needs assessment process can help the program designers to do each of the following, EXCEPT to

    A. identify which programs to implement first
    B. identify the types of programs needed
    C. establish a set of baseline data to demonstrate later improvements
    D. establish incentives for behavioral change

4. The most common mistake health educators make in designing a worksite wellness program is to

    A. depend solely on a schedule of classes for health improvement intervention
    B. focus only on at-risk employees
    C. use the "menu approach" to offering a variety of programs
    D. spend too much time tracking down employees to persuade them to take part in programs or classes

5. A health educator working in a Hispanic/Latino community should remember that the diverse Hispanic cultures in America tend to share some common values and behaviors. Which of the following is NOT one of these?

    A. Family as the primary source of emotional and psychological support.
    B. Matriarchal family structures.
    C. Consultation with several family members before seeking health care.
    D. Modesty and personal privacy.

6. Which of the following interventions does NOT conform to the medical model of health education?

    A. Persuading parents to bring their children in for vaccinations
    B. Teaching a course on how to care for teeth and gums
    C. Participating in a self-help group to discuss the issue of menopause
    D. Screening middle-aged men for high blood pressure

7. Of the following, which element should typically appear FIRST in the body of a proposal for the funding of a public health education program?

    A. The specific methods that will be used to meet program objectives-approach, action plan, timeline
    B. Process and outcome measures to be used in evaluating project success
    C. Brief background of the problem in the community, with supporting data
    D. The management plan for the project, including key staff members and their roles

8. At the local high school, a health educator is conducting a workshop on the dangers of certain commonly abused drugs to a group of Asian immigrant parents. The health educator is aware that English is a second language for many of the parents. Each of the following is a strategy that will help the educator overcome this language barrier in presenting information, EXCEPT

    A. speaking more loudly
    B. using images, gestures, and simple written instructions that may be understood by relatives
    C. speaking slowly and enunciating clearly
    D. repeating sentences in the same words if it's been misunderstood

9. A person who takes the structuralist view of behavior and social change will probably focus his or her efforts on the

    A. laws, codes, zoning ordinances, and taxation of the community
    B. sense of shared purpose among community members
    C. biomedical causes of a disease or disorder
    D. individual's motivation for change

10. When defining and organizing a written message for an adult audience with limited reading skills, a health educator's sentences should

    A. include vivid descriptive phrases to add interest
    B. average 8 to 10 words in length
    C. have roughly the same rhythm
    D. be written in the passive voice

11. In researching a community profile, most of the information can be obtained from the data collected by the

    A. local hospitals
    B. state and local social service departments
    C. chambers of commerce
    D. federal Bureau of the Census

12. When deciding whether to use visuals as part of health instruction, the primary consideration should be whether they

    A. enhance the message, rather than compete with it
    B. illustrate key concepts
    C. stimulate learner interest
    D. are culturally appropriate

13. The probability for learning in a health education program is likely to be enhanced when the following principles are used in program design:
    I. Program content is relevant to the learner, and is perceived by the learner to be relevant.
    II. Instructional methods that stimulate the widest variety of senses will generally be most effective.
    III. Concepts should be reviewed and repeated several times during instruction.
    IV. Instruction should move from the unknown to the known.

    A. I and IV
    B. I, II and III
    C. II and III
    D. I, II, III and IV

14. Which of the following is MOST likely to be a kind of formative evaluation used for a health education program?

    A. Studies of public behavior/health change
    B. Assessment of target audience for knowledge gain
    C. Calculation of percentage of target audience participating
    D. Focus group

15. In social marketing theory, the best example of a "channel gatekeeper" would be a

    A. mother of a large urban family
    B. postal carrier
    C. human resources manager at a large corporation
    D. social worker specializing in substance abuse

16. A health agency plans to publish its own nutrition handbook. Guidelines for the visual design of such a publication include
    I. Concepts that belong together or have similarities should be boxed in.
    II. Narrow columns, rather than full-page-wide text, should be used.
    III. When paragraphs are short, do not indent
    IV. If possible, margins should be wider at the bottom than at the top of the page.

    A. I only
    B. I and IV
    C. II and III
    D. I, II, III and IV

17. Which of the following is NOT a risk factor associated with cirrhosis?

    A. Infectious agents
    B. High blood cholesterol

C. Alcohol abuse
D. Biological factors

18. Which of the following types of funding is MOST likely to be awarded for a program that originates with the funding source?

    A. Grant
    B. Public funds
    C. Private funds
    D. Contract

19. The PROCEED model of planning health education programs adds each of the following procedures to the PRECEDE model, EXCEPT assessment of

    A. budgetary and staff resources required
    B. barriers to overcome in delivering health education
    C. predisposing, enabling, and reinforcing factors among community members
    D. policies that can be used to support the program

20. Theatrical or dramatization exercises are sometimes a useful means of instruction in health education. Generally, a disadvantage associated with this activity is that it

    A. may make some participants uncomfortable
    B. stimulates participants' emotions
    C. distracts from the real purpose of the program
    D. may make issues seem artificial or contrived

21. Which of the following questions would be MOST likely to appear in the formative evaluation of a health education program?

    A. Did the media organizations that the agency contacted change their practices to include photos of safe bicycling?
    B. How many agency-sponsored activities received coverage in the local press?
    C. How many members actively monitored the local media on a regular basis?
    D. How many parents were influenced to buy bicycle helmets after reading the agency's press releases?

22. A health educator wants to draw attention to a new program by placing an op-ed piece about AIDS awareness in the local newspaper. The ideal length for such a piece would be about _____ words.

    A. 100
    B. 300
    C. 800
    D. 1200

23. Of the following areas for change, most nationwide initiatives focusing on public health, such as Healthy People 2000, place the highest priority on

    A. alcohol and other drugs
    B. nutrition
    C. maternal and infant health
    D. food and drug safety

24. Problems or shortcomings associated with the client-centered approach to health education include:
    I. Clients tend to overemphasize environmental determinants of health, such as socio-economic conditions and unemployment.
    II. Clients' prior experience may have led them to need and want professional leadership.
    III. Choices of materials and methods usually involve some sort of value judgement on the part of the health educator.
    IV. There may be a conflict between the identified concerns of a client and those of the professional.

    A. I and II
    B. II and IV
    C. III only
    D. I, II, III and IV

25. In conducting a community assessment, advantages associated with focus group interviews include
    I. potential use as a marketing tool
    II. teaching and learning taking place on many levels
    III. possible function as support group for some members
    IV. increased likelihood of candid, unbiased assessments

    A. In only
    B. I, II and III
    C. II and IV
    D. I, II, III and IV

KEY (CORRECT ANSWERS)

1.	C	11.	D
2.	A	12.	A
3.	D	13.	B
4.	A	14.	D
5.	B	15.	C
6.	C	16.	D
7.	C	17.	B
8.	A	18.	D
9.	A	19.	C
10.	B	20.	A

21.	C
22.	C
23.	B
24.	B
25.	B

TEST 3

DIRECTIONS: Each question or incomplete statement is followed by several suggested answers or completions. Select the one the BEST answers the question or completes the statement. *PRINT THE LETTER OF THE CORRECT ANSWER IN THE SPACE AT THE RIGHT.*

1. From a health education perspective, the key to developing strategies for risk reduction in a community is/are the   1.____

   A. receptiveness of the community to intervention
   B. particular health risks generally associated with the community
   C. geographic and hygienic factors in the community
   D. shared values and institutions of the community

2. As a funding source for health education programs, foundations usually   2.____

   A. provide annual reports and funding guidelines on request
   B. provide gifts in kind
   C. don't specify what kind of projects will be funded
   D. don't fund projects requesting 100 percent funding

3. A health educator who takes a holistic approach to service delivery is probably more likely than traditional practitioners to make use of   3.____

   A. existing government structures and programs
   B. translators or community liaisons
   C. secondary health education
   D. natural support systems

4. A health agency has composed a 15-second public service announcement to be aired on local television. The agency wants to learn how and whether the announcement stands out among the clutter of other messages broadcast each day. Assuming adequate resources, the best possible pre-test for the PSA would be   4.____

   A. self-administered questionnaires
   B. focus groups
   C. theater testing
   D. individual interviews

5. At a bare minimum, a comprehensive health promotion program at a major worksite should include each of the following activities, EXCEPT   5.____

   A. group weight loss programs
   B. exercise and fitness programs
   C. nutrition counseling
   D. health risk appraisals

6. A health educator is in the process of recruiting workers at an automobile manufacturing plant for a wellness program. The educator should know that the most effective way to involve blue-collar workers in a worksite program is to avoid   6.____

11

A. one-on-one counseling or guided self-help
B. setting up screening stations where large numbers of employees work in the production area or the lunchroom, for example
C. a reliance on formal classes for reducing specific health risks
D. attempting to make any changes to the worksite itself

7. In sociology, the _____ theory suggests that society tends toward conservatism and maintenance of the status quo.

    A. exchange
    B. conflict
    C. innovation-diffusion
    D. consensus

8. When evaluating the success of a health education program, an agency should

    A. coordinate the evaluation effort with all phases of the program and all levels of personnel
    B. select the most thorough evaluation possible
    C. opt for sophisticated and complex evaluation approaches
    D. generally ignore subjective inputs from participants

9. Usually, the most effective and efficient way of overcoming a language barrier between a health educator and a group of clients is to

    A. learn the client language in order to interact more personably with them
    B. train and use bilingual community members for use in programs
    C. provide a course in English "survival" skills for clients
    D. seek the help of a health care professional who is fluent in the client language

10. A health educator plans to use headings as an organizational tool in her food safety brochure. Which of the following statements about the use of headings in printed material is generally FALSE?

    A. For competent readers, headings are most effective when used with long paragraphs.
    B. Visuals with headings allow readers to react before more detailed information is given.
    C. One-word headings are more instructional and eye-catching than brief explanatory phrases.
    D. Captions or headings should summarize and emphasize important information.

11. Of the following visual tools for instruction or promotion, which is generally LEAST likely to influence behavior change?

    A. Flipchart
    B. Poster
    C. Talk board
    D. Model

12. In planning a health education program, a group states the goals of its planning process briefly, and then lists in sequence all the steps or activities needed to accomplish the goals. Target data for program implementation is established, and a timetable for each phase of the process is developed. The best way to visually represent this process, in order to illustrate task interde-pendencies, is the   12.____

    A. PERT chart
    B. decision tree
    C. Gantt chart
    D. nomograph

13. Each of the following is an example of primary health education, EXCEPT a course in   13.____

    A. contraception
    B. quitting smoking
    C. personal relationships
    D. nutrition

14. A correlational study reveals a strong positive relationship between the amount of time subjects spend at their workplace and the incidence of obesity. One researcher, studying the data, raises the possibility that a tendency to spend long hours at work and obesity may both be the result of a certain slowing of the metabolic processes. This is known as   14.____

    A. bidirectional causation
    B. a longitudinal relationship
    C. the third-variable problem
    D. a multivariate analysis

15. The main problem or shortcoming associated with the social change approach to health education is the   15.____

    A. assumption that "experts" have the "right" answers to complex health problems
    B. political sensitivity of many health issues
    C. lack of community resources available to many clients to reduce health risks
    D. reliance on the value judgements of the health educator

16. When conducting a survey of the community at large, a health educator should   16.____

    A. select respondents based on their potential gain from proposed programs
    B. collect as large a sample as possible and use these data to make final program decisions
    C. consider it a way of increasing community awareness
    D. combine results with data obtained from community opinion leaders

17. Guidelines for the use of visuals as part of health instruction include   17.____
    I. Images of people in the visuals should look like members of the intended audience
    II. Illustrate both desired and undesired behaviors
    III. Avoid diagrams, graphs, and other complicated visuals
    IV. The number of visuals should be limited to emphasize the most important points

A. I only
B. I, III and IV
C. II and III
D. I, II, III and IV

18. Which of the following is a risk factor associated with diabetes?   18._____

   A. Drug abuse
   B. Obesity
   C. Environmental factors
   D. Stress

19. Which of the following questions would be MOST likely to appear in the summative evaluation of a health education program?   19._____

   A. How often did staff and members meet with local media representatives to encourage coverage of the agency's breast-feeding classes?
   B. How many times did the agency submit press releases or letters to the editor?
   C. Which other members of the community besides the local press were notified regarding the agency's breast-feeding classes?
   D. How many mothers attended the breast-feeding classes that were offered by the agency?

20. According to the PATCH model of health education planning developed by the Centers for Disease Control and Prevention, the FIRST step in implementing a health education program is   20._____

   A. mobilizing the community
   B. choosing health priorities
   C. enhancement of community awareness about the program
   D. developing a comprehensive intervention strategy

21. When making a comparison of mortality rates by race, sex, and age groups, a health educator will need to aggregate _____ of data, unless the community is a large   21._____

   A. 6 to 12 months
   B. 12 to 18 months
   C. 3 to 5 years
   D. 5 to 10 years

22. A health educator is asked by the agency director to write a public service announcement to be aired on the radio. The agency has purchased a 20-second spot. The PSA should be about _____ words in length.   22._____

   A. 20-25
   B. 30-35
   C. 40-50
   D. 60-75

23. Professional standards for implementing health education programs at the local level include each of the following principles and guidelines, EXCEPT   23._____

   A. an emphasis on health outcomes
   B. a fill-in-the-blanks approach to allow communities to establish objectives

C. a focus on professional practice standards, rather than programs
D. the importance of negotiating responsibilities between state and local agencies

24. A health educator decides that in conducting a seminar for elderly Asian-American women on the risk factors associated with osteoporosis, she will adopt a permissive communication style. A potential disadvantage associated with this decision is that clients may

    A. conform to other people's ideas, rather than develop their own
    B. become fearful and reluctant to take independent action
    C. lose self-respect and motivation to change
    D. not receive important advice or information unless they ask for it

25. As a mass media channel for the communication of a health-related message or public service announcement, newspapers

    A. are most likely to reach audiences who do not typically use the health care system
    B. can be used to more specifically target segments of the public
    C. involve strict government regulation concerning the content of public service messages
    D. usually involve the most thorough coverage, but the smallest likelihood of audience attention

KEY (CORRECT ANSWERS)

1.	D	11.	B
2.	A	12.	A
3.	D	13.	B
4.	C	14.	C
5.	A	15.	B
6.	C	16.	C
7.	D	17.	B
8.	A	18.	B
9.	B	19.	D
10.	C	20.	A

21. C
22. C
23. C
24. D
25. D

EXAMINATION SECTION
TEST 1

DIRECTIONS: Each question or incomplete statement is followed by several suggested answers or completions. Select the one that BEST answers the question or completes the statement. *PRINT THE LETTER OF THE CORRECT ANSWER IN THE SPACE AT THE RIGHT.*

1. In the binary system (using digits 0 and 1), the decimal system number 232 is written as

    A. 1010101 B. 1110100 C. 11101000 D. 11101010

2. The following data is for a firm selling cigarettes, cigars, and pipe tobacco for the year 2019, and the average for the base years 2017-19.

	Quantity in 2017-19	2019	Price in 2017-19	2019
Cigarettes	7,000	8,000	2.20	2.50
Cigars	1,100	1,000	3.10	3.40
Pipe tobacco	900	1,000	0.90	0.80

    The 2019 index number (2017-19 = 100) for total sales is

    A. 123 B. 120 C. 112 D. 110

3. Given the following data:

	Country A		Country B
Age Group	Population	Death Rate Per 1,000	Population
0-24	1,200,000	1.7	2,400,000
25-64	2,500,000	7.2	3,000,000
65 and over	300,000	125.0	600,000

    If the death rates in each age group in Country B are the same as in Country A, then the ratio of the total crude death rate in Country A over that for Country B is MOST NEARLY

    A. .80 B. .86 C. 1.17 D. 1.20

4. If $B(m,n) = \int_0^1 x^{m-1}(1-x)^{n-1}\,dx$ and $x = (1+y)^{-1}$, then $B(m,n)$ in terms of y equals

    A. $\int_0^\infty \frac{y^{n-1}dy}{(1+y)^{m+n}}$

    B. $\int_0^\infty -\frac{y^{m-1}dy}{(1+y)^{m+n}}$

    C. $\int_0^1 \frac{y^m\,dy}{(1+y)^{m+n-2}}$

    D. $\int_0^\infty \frac{y^{m-1}\,dy}{(1+y)^{m+n-2}}$

5. If there are n values of X_i and Y_i, and ξX_i and ξY_i stands for the sum of all values from $i = 1$ to $i = n$, and $\bar{X} = \xi \frac{X}{n}i$ and $\bar{Y} = \frac{Y}{n}i$, then the $\xi\,(X_i - X)(Y_i - Y)$ equals

A. $\xi X_i Y_i - n\overline{XY}$
B. $n\xi X_i Y_i - \xi X_i \xi Y_i$
C. $\xi X_i Y_i - \xi X_i \xi Y_i$
D. $\xi X_i Y_i - 3\overline{XY}$

6. Given the Cogg-Douglas function: $x = a l^b k^c$. Assume X = log x, A = log a, B = log b, K = log k, L = log 1, C = log c, then X =

   A. a + bL + CK
   B. A + BL + CK
   C. A·B·C·L·K
   D. A + bL + cK

7. When the forecast of the meteorologist at the Weather Bureau is based on the compilation of all available meteorological data is indicative of the strength of his belief as an expert, this MOST directly exemplifies the _____ approach to probability.

   A. classical
   B. conditional
   C. relative frequency
   D. subjective

8. A sample of 8 students from a class of 40 are selected at random and 5 are boys and 3 are girls. The probability of this result, if it is known that there are 20 girls in the class, is

   A. .375 B. .237 C. .23 D. .21

9. A department head calls in three of his bureau chiefs to help him determine whether or not to make a certain decision. From past experience, he knows that two of his bureau chiefs are wrong 5 percent of the time and that the third is wrong 10 percent of the time. He decides to make the decision proposed by the majority. His decision will then be wrong _____ percent of the time.

   A. 0.25 B. 0.5 C. 1.2 D. 6.7

10. The performances of an experienced stock market analyst is being studied. From past records we determine that when he predicts the market will rise, it rises 70 percent of the time and when he predicts it will fall, it falls 80 percent of the time. If during the period in question the market is rising 90 percent of the time, the posterior probability that the market will actually fall on a day that he predicts a drop is

    A. .20 B. .23 C. .30 D. .31

11. In consumer sampling, if we have reason to believe that there are important differences in consumer attitudes according to age and sex, then the sampling procedure that would probably be MOST desirable is the _____ sample.

    A. cluster
    B. simple random
    C. stratified
    D. systematic

12. In the conduct of a survey, statistical theory provides the bases by which the senior statistician can BEST

    A. determine how the nonsampling errors affect the results
    B. determine the sampling errors that result from a probability sample of the preselected frame
    C. evaluate the content of the questionnaire
    D. go from the frame to the universe

13. In a complicated systematic, stratified, cluster sampling design, the BEST and SIMPLEST formulas for the standard error can be obtained from the theory of

    A. cohort analysis
    B. multi-stage sampling
    C. replicated sampling
    D. sequential sampling

14. If a die is thrown 105 times, then the sum of the expected mean plus the standard deviation of the mean equals MOST NEARLY

    A. 6 1/12   B. 6 5/12   C. 3 1/2   D. 3 2/3

15. The size of the sample that is required to determine whether a Democrat or Republican will win a certain election within .3 percent accuracy with 95.4 percent confidence is

    A. 1,000   B. 1,111   C. 10,329   D. 11,111

16. In a cluster sample, it is desirable that each cluster be

    A. heterogeneous and the differences between clusters be homogeneous
    B. homogeneous and the different clusters be heterogeneous
    C. homoscedastic and the different clusters be hetero-scedastastic
    D. just like every other cluster

Questions 17-18.

DIRECTIONS: Questions 17 and 18 are to be answered on the basis of the following information.

Given the following population:
- Stratum I: 3, 4, 4, 6, 6, 7
- Stratum II: 8, 8, 12, 15, 17, 18
- Stratum III: 16, 16, 18, 22, 22, 26

and the interview cost in Stratum I is $1 per interview, $4 for Stratum II, and $9 for Stratum III.

17. A sample of size n = 10 selected by optimum allocation would have the following sample from each stratum:

    A. 3, 5, 2   B. 3, 4, 3   C. 2, 5, 3   D. 2, 4, 4

18. If the variance of $\bar{X}$ in the above question is given by the formula,

    $$V(\bar{X}) = \sum_{k=1}^{k=3} \frac{N_k - n_k}{N_k - 1} = \frac{(N_k S_k)^2}{n_k}$$

    where N_k is the universe number in stratum nk, k = the number sampled and S_k is the standard deviation in stratum k, then $V(\bar{X})$ equals MOST NEARLY

    A. 1.08   B. 10.8   C. 10.9   D. 180

19. In an investigation of the effect of diet on the incidence of heart disease, a senior statistician made a detailed survey of 1,000 men selected at random over a 10-year period. The group received regular, thorough, physical examinations. The senior statistician concluded that the diet lowered the cholesterol level of all members of the group. His investigation is MOST seriously defective since he

A. had no control group for comparison
B. did not show in his results that the incidence of heart disease was lowered
C. did not show that his group did not develop other serious illnesses
D. did not compute the sampling errors

20. A 30 percent response was secured after 5 mailings in a nationwide follow-up sample survey of 30,000 persons who graduated from high school 5 years before. Under these circumstances, the statistician in charge of this survey should BEST recommend that

    A. substitution of other graduates in the same areas be made and mail questionnaires sent to the substitutes
    B. the survey should be scrapped
    C. the 9,000 returns are adequate and should be used as the final report
    D. an intensive follow-up by telephone and personal visit be made of 5 percent of the nonrespondents

21. One way to determine the extent of interviewer bias is to compute $\sim$ - the average intra-class correlation between interviews within investigators. If g is the number of interviews per investigator, then Var $(\bar{X}) = \frac{G2}{g}[(1+\sim(g-1)]$, where without such bias Var $(\bar{X}) = \frac{G2}{g}$.

    Assuming that each investigator does 101 interviews and $\sim$ = .03, then a self-filled questionnaire sample without interviewer bias would give the same results as an interviewer sample of _____ percent.

    A. 50 B. 33 1/3 C. 25 D. 10

22. In many sample research studies, the investigator compares the results for a control group and an experimental group solely in terms of the differences between the averages of the 2 groups. This procedure is defective PRIMARILY because

    A. both measures may contain biases
    B. differences may frequently result from the presence of sampling errors
    C. small differences are statistically significant
    D. the sampling designs are faulty

23. A common method to check on the validity of a sample is to check some characteristic against known total figures obtained from a complete count, such as a census or an accounting tabulation. This is NOT a valid test because

    A. the greater detailed tabulations obtained from the sample makes it easier to spot inaccuracies
    B. the size of the universe determines the size of the sample
    C. the nonsampling errors in a complete count are frequently greater than the sampling plus nonsampling errors of the sample
    D. modern computing machines eliminate most of the non-sampling errors in samples

24. A research survey is to be made by a team of psychologists and you are the consulting senior statistician. Your functions will MOST likely include the

    A. decision as to whether or not the proposed frame is satisfactory
    B. determination of the type of statistical information to be obtained
    C. rules for coding the data and the actual coding
    D. selection of the sample and the computation of estimates and standard errors

25. A survey was made in 22 cities before and after a heavy advertising campaign for a certain product. The results showed that about 71.9 percent were aware of the product before advertising and 74.2 percent afterwards. About 1,000 persons were interviewed by telephone before and a different 1,000 persons after the campaign. The non-response rate was about 60 percent in each case. From this statement of the project, it can be said that

    A. the difference of 2.3 percent is significant
    B. a smaller sample would have produced better results
    C. no valid probability statement can be made of the effectiveness of the advertising
    D. nothing could be done about the non-response

KEY (CORRECT ANSWERS)

1.	C	11.	C
2.	A	12.	B
3.	B	13.	C
4.	A	14.	D
5.	A	15.	B
6.	D	16.	A
7.	D	17.	A
8.	C	18.	C
9.	C	19.	A
10.	B	20.	D

21. C
22. B
23. C
24. D
25. C

SOLUTIONS TO PROBLEMS

1. CORRECT ANSWER: C
   In the binary system, counting from right to left, the placeholders are 1, 2, 4, 8, 16, 32, 64, 128,.... Since 232 = (1)(128) + (1)(64) + (1)(32) + (0)(16) + (1)(8) + (0)(4) + (0)(2) + (0)(1), the binary form of 232 is 11101000.

2. CORRECT ANSWER: A
   The total sales for 2017-19 = (7000)(2.20) + (1100)(3.10) + (900)(.90) = $19,620. The total sales for 2019 = (8000)(2.50) + (1000)(3.40) + (1000)(.80) = $24,200. The index number for 2019 = (24,200/19,620)(100) = 123 (rounded off).

3. CORRECT ANSWER: B
   Country A
   Population: 1,200,000 + 2,500,000 + 300,000 = 4,000,000
   Deaths:

   $$1,200,000 \times \frac{1.7}{1000} = 2,040$$

   $$2,500,000 \times \frac{7.2}{1000} = 18,000$$

   $$300,000 \times \frac{125}{1000} = 37,500$$

   Total = 57,540

   Total/million: $\frac{57,540}{4} = 14,385$

   Country B
   Population: 2,400,000 + 3,000,000 + 600,000 = 6,000,000
   Deaths:

   $$2,400,000 \times \frac{1.7}{1000} = 4,080$$

   $$3,000,000 \times \frac{7.2}{1000} = 21,600$$

   $$600,000 \times \frac{125}{1000} = 75,000$$

   Total = 100,680

   Total/million: $\frac{100,680}{6} = 16,780$

   $$\frac{\text{Death rate country A}}{\text{Death rate country B}} = \frac{14,385}{16780} = .857 = .86$$

4. CORRECT ANSWER: A

$$B(m,n) = \int_0^1 x^{m-1}(1-x)^{n-1} dx \qquad x = (1+y)^{-1}, \text{ then}$$

B(m,n) in terms of y equals

	x=0	x=1
$x = \dfrac{1}{1+y}$	$(1+y)^{-1} = 0$	$(1+y)^{-1} = 1$
$dx = \dfrac{1}{(1+y)^2} dy$	$\dfrac{1}{1+y} = 0$	$\dfrac{1}{1+y} = 1$
$x^{m-1} = \left(\dfrac{1}{1+y}\right)^{m-1} = \dfrac{(1+y)}{(1+y)^m}$	$y + 1 = \dfrac{1}{0} = \infty$	$y = 0$
$(1-x)^{n-1} = \left[1 - \left(\dfrac{1}{1+y}\right)\right]^{n-1}$	$y = \infty$	
$= \left[\dfrac{y}{1+y}\right]^{n-1}$		

$$B(m,n) = \int_\infty^0 \dfrac{(1+y)}{(1+y)^m} \cdot \dfrac{y^{n-1}}{(1+y)^{n-1}} \cdot \dfrac{(-1)1}{(1+y)^2} dy$$

$$= \int_\infty^0 \dfrac{y^{n-1} dy}{(1+y)^{m+n}}$$

5. CORRECT_ANSWER: A

$\xi (X_i - \overline{X})(Y_i - \overline{Y}) = \xi (X_iY_i) - \xi \overline{X} Y_i - \xi Y\overline{X}_i + \xi \overline{XY}$

$= \xi X_iY_i - \overline{X}\xi Y_i - \overline{Y}\xi X_i + n\overline{XY}$

$= \xi X_iY_i - n\overline{XY} - n\overline{XY} + n\overline{XY} = \xi X_iY_i - n\overline{XY}$

6. CORRECT ANSWER: D

$a\tilde{\ell}^b k^c$, so $\log x = X = \text{Log}[a\ell^b k^c]$

$= \text{Log } a + b\text{Log } \ell + c\text{Log } k = A + bL + cK$

7. CORRECT ANSWER: D
Whenever a person utilizes his personal belief on a question involving probability, this illustrates a subjective approach.

8. CORRECT ANSWER: C

$$\dfrac{20C_5 \cdot 20C_3}{40C_8} = 2298$$

$$\text{Numerator} = \dfrac{20 \times 19 \times 18 \times 17 \times 16 \times 20 \times 19 \times 18}{5 \times 4 \times 3 \times 2 \ \times \ 3 \times 2 \times 1}$$

$$= \dfrac{19 \times 3 \times 17 \times 16 \times 20 \times 19 \times 3}{19}$$

Denominator $= \dfrac{40 \times 39 \times 38 \times 37 \times 36 \times 35 \times 34 \times 33}{2 \times 7 \times 6 \times 5 \times 4 \times 3 \times 2 \times 1} = .2298$

9. CORRECT ANSWER: C
   Assume that the first two chiefs are wrong .05 of the time and the third chief is wrong .10 of the time. P (wrong decision for dept. head) = P (1st chief wrong) P (2nd chief wrong) P (3rd chief right) + P (1st chief wrong) P (2nd chief right) - P (3rd chief wrong) + P (1st chief right) P (2nd chief wrong) P (3rd chief wrong) + P (all 3 chiefs wrong) = $(.05)^2(.90)$ + $(.05)(.95)(.10) + (.95)(.05)(.10) + (.05)^2(.10) = .012$.

10. CORRECT ANSWER: B
    We have P(A|B) = .70, P(A'|B) = .30, P(B) = .90, P(B') = .10, where A = predicts market will rise, B = market does rise, A' = predicts market will fall, B' = market does fall. We also know that P(A'|B') = .80. Then, P(B'|A') = P(B')·P(A'|B')/ [P(B')·P(A'|B') + P(B) P(A'|B)] =

    $(.10)(.80)/[(.10)(.80) + (.90)(.30)] = .08/.35 \approx .23$.

11. CORRECT ANSWER: C
    In this type of sampling, the actual sample is selected from specific categories, such as age and sex. The sample would include both genders and individuals of different ages.

12. CORRECT ANSWER: B
    In any statistically-related surveys, errors will occur. The statistician must be able to identify these errors, by way of statistical theory.

13. CORRECT ANSWER: C
    Replication permits estimating the experimental error and also provides for minimizing it. This type of sampling yields best results for a standard error.

14. CORRECT ANSWER: D
    The mean = 1(1/6) + 2(1/6) + 3(1/6) + 4(1/6) + 5(1/6) + 6(1/6) = 3.5. The standard deviation of the mean =

    $\sqrt{(0^2 \cdot 1/6 + 1^2 \cdot 1/6 + 2^2 \cdot 1/6 + 3^2 \cdot 1/6 + 4^2 \cdot 1/6 + 5^2 \cdot 1/6 + 6^2 \cdot 1/6 - (3.5)^2]/105}$ = $.1\overline{6}$ = .16.
    So, $3.5 + .1\overline{6} = 3\ 2/3$

15. CORRECT ANSWER: B
    Z, -6 The formula is $n = \left(\dfrac{Z_{\alpha/2} \cdot \delta}{E}\right)^2$, where n = required number,

    $Z_{\alpha/2}$ = critical Z value of a normal distribution, δ = standard deviation, and E = error.

    Thus, $n = \left(\dfrac{2 \cdot \frac{1}{2}}{.03}\right)^2 = (33.\overline{3})^2 \approx 1111$. We assume that $\delta = \dfrac{1}{2}$.

16. CORRECT ANSWER: A
    In cluster sampling, each cluster will represent a cross-section of a desired trait. However, all clusters will share these cross-sections.

17. **CORRECT ANSWER: A**
    The expected value of any sample of each strata are:
    $E \bar{X}_I = 5$, $E \bar{X}_{II} = 13$, $E \bar{X}_{III} = 20$. The expected cost for
    stratum I = ($1)(5)(13) + ($4)(13)(5) + ($9)(20)(2) = $635, wich choice A. This is lower than the values of choices B, C, or D, which are respectively $763, $810, and $938.

18. **CORRECT ANSWER: C**

19. **CORRECT ANSWER: A**
    A control group is necessary in order to make sound comparisons.

20. **CORRECT ANSWER: D**
    This procedure would raise the response rate to 35%, which should yield a fairly accurate set of results.

21. **CORRECT ANSWER: C**
    With bias on the part of the interviewer, $V(\bar{X}) = \dfrac{\delta^2}{100}[1+ (.03)(100)]$
    $= \dfrac{4\delta^2}{100} = \delta^2/25$. Without bias, $V(\bar{X}) = \delta^2/100$. The ratio of $\delta^2/100 \div \delta^2/25$ reduces to 1/4 or 25%.

22. **CORRECT ANSWER: B**
    This is especially true if random sampling was used, because any outliers would definitely affect the value of the average.

23. **CORRECT ANSWER: C**
    Whereas sampling errors are due to a poor sampling plan which does not contain a truly accurate picture of the population, non-sampling errors are the result of inaccurate observations. The latter type of errors of a population would normally exceed, in count, both types of errors for any particular sample.

24. **CORRECT ANSWER: D**
    The statistician is more concerned with sample selection and subsequent analysis than with methods of coding data or with the type of data being sought.

25. **CORRECT ANSWER: C**
    Since only about 400 people responded, the actual numbers represented by 71.9% and 74.2% are 288 and 297, respectively. This is hardly significant, with 600 non-respondents.

TEST 2

DIRECTIONS: Each question or incomplete statement is followed by several suggested answers or completions. Select the one that BEST answers the question or completes the statement. *PRINT THE LETTER OF THE CORRECT ANSWER IN THE SPACE AT THE RIGHT.*

1. If you had to determine the extent and impact of automation in a metropolitan city industry, the BEST way to proceed would be to

    A. do a two-stage sample survey. The first stage would be a comprehensive, sample mail survey to determine the presence of the equipment and the second stage would involve intensive interviewing of those who reported that they had such equipment
    B. do a comprehensive library research job of the literature for instances of the uses of automation in this city and then do a field follow-up of those firms that have it
    C. study all previous surveys and do an intensive job in those industries and size groups where automation may be prevalent
    D. design a detailed, comprehensive questionnaire and send it to all firms in this city

2. A certain drug is known to produce nausea in about 1 percent of the patients in the general population. A doctor gave this drug to 100 of his patients with a certain disease and since none of them complained of nausea, he concluded that the drug was perfectly safe to use. His conclusions were invalid in that such a result would obtain only for samples of 100 about _____ percent of the time.

    A. 10   B. 37   C. 63   D. 95

    NOTE: Use the Poisson distribution $\frac{m^x e^{-m}}{x!}$, where $m = N \cdot p$ and $e = 2.718$.

3. If $r_{12.3} = \frac{r_{12} - r_{13} r_{23}}{\sqrt{(1-r_{13}^2)(1-r_{23}^2)}}$ and $r_{12} = .3$, $r_{13} = .1$, and $r_{23} = .5$ than $r_{12.3}$ equals

    A. .29   B. .31   C. .42   D. .65

4. If $r_{12} = r_{23} = r_{34} = \sim$ and $r_{13} = r_{24} = \sim^2$, and $r_{14} = \sim^3$, then the partial correlation coefficients $r_{13.2}$, $r_{14.2}$, $r_{24.3}$ and $r_{14.3}$ are all

    A. equal to 0
    B. except $r_{14.3}$ equal to 0
    C. except $r_{13.2}$ equal to 1
    D. equal to 1

5. If the seasonal index for a time series is 120 in a given month, this means that the

    A. average of the seasonal indices for the other 11 months is 80
    B. seasonal index for that month is higher than at least half of the other months
    C. seasonal index for at least one other month must be below 100
    D. unadjusted data for the month is increased 20 percent when seasonally adjusted

6. If an employment series is declining over a period of time, then the linear regression equation (y = a+bt) where it is positive for all years MUST have

    A. a negative a and positive b
    B. a positive a and negative b
    C. either a positive or negative a and a negative b
    D. either a positive or negative a and a positive or negative b

7. The one of the following statements concerning the normal distribution which is false is that the

    A. normal distribution has exceptionally convenient properties which have made it the model for much of statistical theory
    B. normal distribution is the one unifying model for the representation of the random variation in all measurable natural phenomena
    C. many non-normal distributions approach normality under certain limiting conditions which can be frequently simulated in practical situations
    D. random variation of many natural phenomena can be represented by the normal distribution to a high degree of accuracy

8. In testing the hypothesis that r means are equal, of the following, the analysis of variance technique does NOT assume that

    A. an equal number of observations be made from each of the r populations
    B. the r samples are drawn randomly
    C. the r populations are normal
    D. the r population variances are equal

9. Given the matrix of simple correlations,

$$R = \begin{vmatrix} r_{11} & r_{12} & r_{13} \\ r_{12} & r_{22} & r_{23} \\ r_{13} & r_{23} & r_{33} \end{vmatrix}$$

    and that the multiple coefficient of determination $R^2_{123} = 1 - R/R_{11}$, where R is the value of the above determinant and R_{11} is the cofactor of r_{11}, which equals $1 - r^2_{23}$, if $r_{11} = r_{22} = r_{33} = 1$ and $r_{12} = .5$, $r_{13} = -.5$, and $r_{23} = 0$, then $R^2_{1.23}$ equals

    A. 0   B. 1/3   C. 1/4   D. 1/2

10. To test the hypothesis that the number of storks and the birth rate are independent, the following data have been gathered:

	Number of Storks		
Countries With	Few	Many	Total
Small birth rate	50	10	60
Large birth rate	150	40	190
Total	200	50	250

    The value of x^2 used to test this hypothesis is

    A. .54   B. .55   C. 1.37   D. 5.5

11. The criterion for choosing a point estimator which can be represented by the mean X for the sample approaches u, the mean for the universe as the sample size n approaches the universe size N is that of

    A. unbiasedness
    B. sufficiency
    C. efficiency
    D. consistency

    11.____

12. In a positively skewed distribution of measurements, the _____ is larger than the _____.

    A. mean; median
    B. median; mean
    C. mode; mean
    D. mode; median

    12.____

13. Discriminant analysis is that branch of statistics which attempts to

    A. accept or reject a given hypothesis based on sample data
    B. classify an individual as belonging to one or two populations p_1, or p_2 on the basis of a number of measurements made on him
    C. determine the amount of discrimination prevalent in an area
    D. determine the classification of an individual through his characteristics without error

    13.____

14. A computed chi-square value with a negative sign

    A. has to be interpreted in terms of the defined significance level
    B. always indicates that the observed differences, if any, are significant
    C. always indicates that the observed differences, if any, are insignificant
    D. is mathematically impossible

    14.____

15. In locating the position of the mode within a class of grouped data, it is assumed that the measurements located in the model class are

    A. all located at the midpoint of the class
    B. dispersed according to the frequencies in the two adjoining classes
    C. dispersed equally throughout the class
    D. located at the two class boundaries

    15.____

16. A fisherman decides that he needs a line that will test more than 10 pounds if he is to catch the size fish he desires.
    He tests 16 pieces of Brand F line and finds a sample mean of 10.4. If it is known that the population standard deviation (G) = .5 pound, then the inference statement below that is CORRECT is

    A. Z = 3.2 and the chances are greater than 999 out of 1,000 that $\mu \geq 10$
    B. t = 3.2 and the chances are greater than 99 out of 100 that $\mu \geq 10$
    C. Z = .8 and the chances are only about 39 out of 100 that $\mu \geq 10$
    D. t = .8 and the chances are only 20 out of 100 that $\mu \geq 10$

    16.____

17. A senior statistician in charge of a unit which requires the collection of statistical data from business on a regular basis recommends a method whereby small establishments report quarterly and the larger establishments are required to supply their information monthly. This recommended method applies BEST in circumstances where the burden of reporting is

    17.____

A. geared to the ability of the business to supply the necessary information
B. shared among respondents so that no one business establishment carries a heavier burden than any other
C. partially borne by independent sources such as existing administrative records and the direct collection of information
D. not appreciably affected by reasonable estimations furnished when exact reported information is not supplied

18. Of the following, it is considered MOST likely that productivity will be GREATEST from a group of workers where the supervisor of the group

    A. acts as another employee among the group he supervises
    B. is production-oriented primarily in his approach to supervision
    C. uses the influence he has with his superiors to present employees' legitimate goals
    D. receives emphasis on production from his superiors and, in turn, stresses production from his subordinates

19. Of the following, the basic intent of naming a form is to provide the means to

    A. code those factors recorded on each form
    B. describe the use of the form
    C. index each form
    D. call attention to specific sections within each form

20. In the case where a major project is so complex that it is difficult to comprehend the entire scope of the work involved, it would be BEST in the planning and analysis of such a project to

    A. identify the common elements that are present in most statistical clerical operations
    B. work out a series of checks in the major procedure to indicate any point in the procedure that is not functioning properly
    C. present correlated activities graphically on charts and analyses
    D. consider the entire project as made up of individual minor units

21. Good report writing utilizes, where possible, the use of table of contents, clear titles and subtitles, well-labeled tables and figures, and good summaries in prominent places. These features in a report are MOST helpful in

    A. saving the reader's time
    B. emphasizing objectivity
    C. providing a basic reference tool
    D. forming a basis for future action

22. Of the following types of record forms used in an office, the one that is likely to be obsolete in a relatively short period of time and to require the greater control to prevent the accumulation of unnecessary data is the

    A. external transmittal record
    B. internal transmittal record
    C. journal record
    D. report

23. Assume that you are a supervisor of staff. When your supervisor complains to you concerning a serious error on the part of one of your subordinates, the MOST proper response should be to

    A. state that you cannot do more than spotcheck the work of your subordinates
    B. accept the complaint and report the subordinate for disciplinary action
    C. tell your supervisor that you sincerely hope it will not happen again
    D. assure him that you will check on it to prevent a similar mistake in the future

24. Of the following, the MOST practical way to lessen the problem of monotony in routine work is to

    A. rotate work assignments
    B. assign routine work to the less intelligent
    C. eliminate repetitive tasks
    D. get the subordinate to understand the importance of routine work

25. The CHIEF value of organization charts for the supervisor or administrator is that they

    A. clarify and emphasize the informal but de factor shortcuts in inter-unit communication
    B. clearly outline the lines and levels of responsibility and supervision in the department
    C. prevent the misdirection of inter- and intra-departmental communication
    D. substantially reduce the amount of paper work

KEY (CORRECT ANSWERS)

1. A		11. D	
2. B		12. A	
3. A		13. B	
4. A		14. D	
5. C		15. B	
6. B		16. A	
7. B		17. A	
8. A		18. D	
9. D		19. B	
10. B		20. D	

21. A
22. B
23. D
24. A
25. B

SOLUTIONS TO PROBLEMS

1. **CORRECT ANSWER: A**
   In this fashion, only those respondents who actually had the equipment for automation would be used for further consideration. This procedure is more cost-effective than conducting library research. It is also more efficient time-wise.

2. **CORRECT ANSWER: B**
   Using the Poisson Distribution, $P(X=0) = 1^0 e^{-1} \div 0! = e^{-1} \approx .37$ (Recall $0! = 0$ factorial $= 1$)

3. **CORRECT ANSWER: A**
   $r_{12.3} = [.3 - (.1)(.5)] / \sqrt{(1-.01)(1-.25)}$
   $= .25 / \sqrt{.7425} \approx .29$

4. **CORRECT ANSWER: A**
   It suffices to show that the numerators of the fractions representing each partial correlation coefficient is zero.
   For $r_{13.2}$, the corresponding numerator is $r_{13} - r_{12}r_{23} = p^2 - p.p = 0$. For $r_{14.2}$, the numerator is $r_{14} - r_{12}r_{24} = p^3 - p.p^2 = 0$. For $r_{24.3}$, the numerator is $r_{24} - r_{23}r_{34} = p^2 - p.p = 0$. Finally, for $r_{14.3}$, the numerator is $r_{14} - r_{13}r_{34} = p^3 - p^2.p = 0$.

5. **CORRECT ANSWER: C**
   The index of 100 is assigned to the average of the values of the months under consideration. If one particular month has an index of 120, we can be certain that at least one of the other months must have an index below 100.

6. **CORRECT ANSWER: B**
   Since the value of y is always positive, a must have a positive value. The value of b represents the slope, which is negative due to the fact that the series is declining over a period of time.

7. **CORRECT ANSWER: B**
   Although the Normal Distribution is widely used for many parametric formulas, such as the Poisson and Binomial formulas, it simply does not apply to data which are strictly random, or to non-parametric formulas.

8. **CORRECT ANSWER: A**
   In testing the hypothesis of whether r means are equal, we recognize that ANOVA techniques assume that these populations are normal with equal variances and that they are randomly drawn. ANOVA does NOT insist that each population has the same number of observations.

9. CORRECT ANSWER: D

With substitution, $R = \begin{vmatrix} 1 & .5 & -.5 \\ .5 & 1 & 0 \\ -.5 & 0 & 1 \end{vmatrix}$

$= (1)(1)(1) + (.5)(0)(-.5) + (-.5)(0)(.5) - (-.5)(1)(-.5) - (.5)(.5)(1) - (1)(0)(0) = .5$

$R_{11} = 1 - r^2_{23} = 1 - 0 = 1$

Thus, $R^2_{1.23} = 1 - .5/1 = 1/2$

10. CORRECT ANSWER: B
The expected values of the 4 cells would appear as:

	Few	Many
Small	48	12
Large	152	38

$x^2 = (50-48)^2/48 + (10-12)^2/12 + (150-152)^2/152 + (40-38)^2/38 \approx .548 \approx .55$

11. CORRECT ANSWER: D
A statistic (in this case, x) is considered a consistent estimator of a parameter (in this case, μ) if the probability that the value of x approaching the value of μ increases to 1 as the sample size approaches the population size.

12. CORRECT ANSWER: A
In a positively skewed distribution, the mode is less than the median and the median is less than the mean.

13. CORRECT ANSWER: B
Discriminant analysis generally attempts to classify any subjects being observed into two or more categories (populations) as a direct consequence of observations or measurements that are made. An example with 3 groups would be to identify a voter as Democrat, Republican, or Independent.

14. CORRECT ANSWER: D
By definition, chi-square represents distributions which are ratios of squared values, like $(n-1)s^2/\delta^2$, where n = sample size, δ^2 = population variance, δ^2 = sample variance. Another representation of chi-square would be $\Sigma (O_i - E_i)^2/E_i$, which is a summation of the squared values of differences between observed and expected frequencies divided by expected frequencies. Chi-square must always be non-negative.

15. CORRECT ANSWER: B
In the case of grouped data where a frequency curve has been constructed to fit the data, the mode will be the value (or values) of x corresponding to the maximum point or points on the curve. This value x is sometimes denoted by x .
From a frequency distribution or histogram, the mode can be obtained from the formula:

$$\text{Mode} = L_1 + \left(\frac{\Delta_1}{\Delta_1 + \Delta_2}\right)c$$

L_1 = lower class boundary of modal class (i.e., class containing the mode)

Δ_1 = excess of modal frequency over frequency of next lower class

Δ_2 = excess of modal frequency over frequency of next higher class
c = size of modal class interval.
This justifies answer B dispersed according to the frequencies in the two adjoining classes.

16. CORRECT ANSWER: A
Since the population standard deviation is known, we use the z-score test. $Z = (10.4 - 10)/(.5/\sqrt{16}) = 3.2$. Using the Normal Distribution Table of Z-scores, the probability that $\mu \geq 10$ is very close to .9993.

17. CORRECT ANSWER: A
As a rule, smaller businesses would not have the amount of resources as larger businesses in order to collect statistical data. Thus, the statistician would require the smaller businesses to submit data on a relatively infrequent basis (such as quarterly), whereas he would require the larger businesses to provide the needed data more frequently (such as monthly).

18. CORRECT ANSWER: D
The supervisor will attempt to show his workers that he (the supervisor) has been instructed from higher authority on the importance of production for the company. In this way, the supervised group will acquire a *team spirit* and thus maximize production.

19. CORRECT ANSWER: B
The form's name should be indicative of how the form will be used. Other considerations, like coding, would be secondary.

20. CORRECT ANSWER: D
By dividing up the project into smaller units, there is a much more realistic probability that each unit can be planned and analyzed. At a later stage, material connections can be formulated among several units.

21. CORRECT ANSWER: A
Usually a reader is interested in only a few topics of the report. A well-planned table of contents allows the reader to find those selected topics in a short time, without spending unnecessary time on other topics.

22. CORRECT ANSWER: B
This type of record may consist of very brief reminders or notes, and would be of little value after a period of time.

23. CORRECT ANSWER: D
This is the best course of action to take. Your supervisor needs to be assured that you will do whatever is humanly possible to prevent similar mistakes from re-occurring.

24. CORRECT ANSWER: A
This method affords each individual of performing different tasks within their capabilities.

25. CORRECT ANSWER: B
This describes exactly the purpose of organizational charts.

EXAMINATION SECTION
TEST 1

DIRECTIONS: Each question or incomplete statement is followed by several suggested answers or completions. Select the one that BEST answers the question or completes the statement. *PRINT THE LETTER OF THE CORRECT ANSWER IN THE SPACE AT THE RIGHT.*

1. If $m_x = D/P$, where m_x is the death rate, D is the number of deaths, P is the population; and if q_x, the probability of dying, equals $\dfrac{D}{P+\frac{1}{2}D}$, then the relationship between m_x and q_x is   1.____

    A. $q_x = \dfrac{2m_x}{2+m_x}$
    B. $q_x = \dfrac{m_x}{2+m_x}$
    C. $m_x = \dfrac{2q_x}{2+q_x}$
    D. $m_x = \dfrac{q_x}{1-q_x}$

2. In using the Chi-square technique for testing independence on data arranged in r rows and c columns, the number of degrees of freedom is equal to   2.____

    A. rc - 1
    B. rc + 1
    C. r + c - 1
    D. (r-1)(c-1)

3. If $(1 - R^2_{1.23}) = (1 - r^2_{13})(1 - r^2_{12.3})$ and $r_{13} = r_{12.3} = .5$, then $R_{1.23}$ equals   3.____

    A. .50   B. .56   C. .66   D. .86

4. The infinitely repeating decimal .148514851485... when converted to a fraction in its lowest reduced form is   4.____

    A. 165/1111   B. 15/101   C. 3/20   D. 1/7

5. In order to test the hypothesis that the variances -1^2 and -2^2 of two normally distributed populations are equal, based on two samples with n_1 and n_2 observations, we utilize the statistic   5.____

    A. $F = s_1^2/s_2^2$ and use the F-distribution table with n_1-1 and n_2-1 degrees of freedom
    B. $F = s_1^2/s_2^2$ and use the F-distribution table with n_1 and n_2 degrees of freedom
    C. $X^2 = \dfrac{s_1^2 + s_2^2}{\sigma^2}$ with $n_1 + n_2$ degrees of freedom
    D. $F = \dfrac{n_1 s_1^2}{n_2 s_2^2}$ and use the F-distribution with n_1 and n_2 degrees of freedom

6. Answer this question on the basis of the information given in the table below.

Commodity	Unit	Quantity 2000	Quantity 2005	Price Per Unit 2000	Price Per Unit 2005
Sugar	lb.	40	44	$1.20	$1.40
Flour	pkg.	80	85	$1.70	$1.90
Milk	qt.	25	20	$1.80	$2.20
Bread	loaf	15	20	$1.40	$1.60

The weighted aggregative (Laspeyres) price index for 2005 (2000 = 100) is

A. 114.6   B. 114.7   C. 114.8   D. 114.9

7. The division of 110111 by 1011 in the binary scale gives the following result in the binary scale:

A. 101   B. 110   C. 111   D. 1011

Questions 8-9.

DIRECTIONS: Questions 8 and 9 are to be answered on the basis of the information given below.

In the President's Manpower Report for 2004, a regression analysis was made of the percent change in Gross National Product (G) and Manufacturing Employment (M). The data used were as follows:

G	M
-2	-6.6
0	-4.0
2	-1.5
4	-1.0
6	3.5
8	6.0

(Calculations can be simplified by using deviation from the means.)

8. The regression equation based on the above data is

A. M = -4.29 + 1.23G
B. M = -4.29 - 1.23G
C. G = -4.29 - 1.23M
D. G = 4.29 - 1.23M

9. The correlation between G and M is

A. -.97   B. -.98   C. +.90   D. +.98

10. The Housing Department wishes to make a study of the proportion of buildings that have violations. Assuming that a random sample is to be selected and that with 95 percent confidence a sampling error of 3 percent either way is permitted, how large a sample will be required?

A. 952   B. 1067   C. 1239   D. 2347

11. Suppose there is a bakery that bakes cream cakes every morning. The cakes are such that unless sold every day, they have to be thrown away. For simplicity, assume the maximum number of customers a day is 3, and the maximum number of cakes baked a day is also 3. It costs $2 to bake a cake, and it is sold for $3. Assume that on 20 percent of the days, one customer comes in for a cake, that on 50 percent of the days 2 cakes would be sold, and that on 30 percent of the days 3 cakes would be sold. In order to MAXIMIZE his profits, how many cakes should the baker have on hand?

    A. 0 B. 1 C. 2 D. 3

12. A test to detect cancer is discovered that proves to be 95 percent reliable. If given to people who have cancer, the test will be positive 95 percent of the time and negative 5 percent of the time; if given to people who do not have cancer, the test will be negative 95 percent of the time and positive 5 percent of the time. Suppose this test is given to a large group of persons of whom 0.5 percent have cancer. Which of the following expresses MOST NEARLY the probability that a person with a positive test really has cancer?

    A. .95 B. .91 C. .09 D. .05

13. Answer this question on the basis of the table given below.

	PLANT A		PLANT B	
Age	Workers	Days Lost	Workers	Days Lost
20-29	100	600	400	2400
30-39	200	1600	400	3200
40-49	400	4000	100	1000
50+	400	4800	100	1200

    In a study of absenteeism caused by sickness in two different plants, the average days lost were 10 per man in Plant A and 7.8 per man in Plant B. Upon further analysis of the data above on which these averages were based, the statistician concluded that

    A. standardizing the rates by age group results in no difference in the averages
    B. the difference is not statistically significant
    C. in addition to the averages, the variations in the data should be presented
    D. A X^2 test should be used to determine the significance of the differences

14. One version of the Law of Large Numbers states that

    $$P[(M-m) \leq \frac{KS}{\sqrt{n}}] = \frac{1}{K^2}$$

    Using this fact, how large a sample (n) is needed at the 5 percent significance level so that the sample mean (m) will be within s/2 of the universe mean (M)?

    A. 160 B. 80 C. 20 D. 5

15. Seventy percent of the firms in a large trade association made a profit last year. The probability that in a simple random sample of 3 firms, exactly 2 out of 3 firms will make a profit is

    A. .33 B. .44 C. .56 D. .67

16. If all samples consisting of two numbers are selected from the population consisting of the numbers 2, 4, 8, 10, then the sum of the mean and variance of the resulting sampling distribution is

    A. 6.8   B. 7.8   C. 9.3   D. 11.0

17. If we add a constant to each observation in a regression problem, y = a + bx, we

    A. do not change the correlation coefficient
    B. change the regression coefficient, b
    C. do not change the value of any part of the regression equation
    D. do not change the value of the constant term, a

18. Heights of army men are normally distributed with a mean of 68 inches and a standard deviation of 3 inches.
    The percent of this population between 65 and 74 inches is MOST NEARLY

    A. 90%   B. 82%   C. 68%   D. 62%

19. As a statistician on a project, you have been assigned to design a punch card. You find that you need 82 columns for your data, but have only 80 columns on the card. You observe that you have assigned three columns to dichotomous data of the yes-no type. The BEST way to solve this dilemma is to

    A. punch the additional two columns on another card since the format for reading the data can easily be adjusted
    B. use a 1-column code for the three columns of dichotomous data based on the binary number system
    C. utilize the X and Y punches on the card
    D. utilize an alphabetic code

20. In testing hypotheses, the probability of a Type 1 error can be made smaller either by increasing the sample size, or by

    A. increasing the Type II error
    B. subtracting Yates' correction factor
    C. utilizing Fisher's z distribution
    D. using a nonparametric test

KEY (CORRECT ANSWERS)

1.	A	11.	C
2.	D	12.	C
3.	C	13.	A
4.	B	14.	B
5.	A	15.	B
6.	C	16.	D
7.	A	17.	A
8.	A	18.	B
9.	D	19.	B
10.	B	20.	A

SOLUTIONS TO PROBLEMS

1. **CORRECT ANSWER: A**
   $q_x = D/(p + 1/2D) = 2D/(2P+D)$
   $= 2Pm_x/(2P+Pm_x$
   $= 2Pm_x/[P(2+m_x)] = 2m_x/(2+m_x)$

2. **CORRECT ANSWER: D**
   With r rows and c columns, (r-1)(c-1) equals the degrees of freedom.

3. **CORRECT ANSWER: C**
   $(1-R^2_{1.23}) = (1-.5^2)(1-.5^2) = .75^2 = .5625$
   Then, $R^2{1.23} = .4375$ and $R_{1.23} \approx .66$

4. **CORRECT ANSWER: B**
   Let $N = \overline{.1485}$, so that $10{,}000N = 1485.\overline{1485}$
   By subtraction, $9999N = 1485$, and $N = 1485/9999$.
   In lowest terms, $N = 15/101$

5. **CORRECT ANSWER: A**
   This test assumes independence of samples. Also, s_1^2 should always be the larger variance.

6. **CORRECT ANSWER: C**
   The base year 2000 calculations $(40)(1.20) + (80)(1.70) + (25)(1.80) + (15)(1.40) = 250.00$
   The 2005 year calculation =
   $(\frac{140}{120})(40)(1.20) + (\frac{190}{170})(80)(1.70) + (\frac{220}{180})(25)(1.80) + (\frac{160}{140})(15)(1.40)$
   $= 287.00$

   The Laspeyres price index = $\frac{287.00}{250.00} \times 100 = 114.8$

7. **CORRECT ANSWER: A**
   $110111_{\text{base 2}} = 32 + 16 + 4 + 2 + 1 = 55_{\text{base 10}}$
   $1011_{\text{base 2}} = 8 + 2 + 1 + = 11_{\text{base 10}}$
   $55/11 = 5 = 101_{\text{base 2}}$

8. **CORRECT ANSWER: A**
   The regression equation is found by solving the following equations: $\sum = 6a + b\sum G$ and $\sum MG = a\sum G + b\sum G^2$. These become: $-3.6 = 6a + 18b$ and $75.2 = 18a + 124b$. Solving, $a = -4.28$ and $b = 1.23$

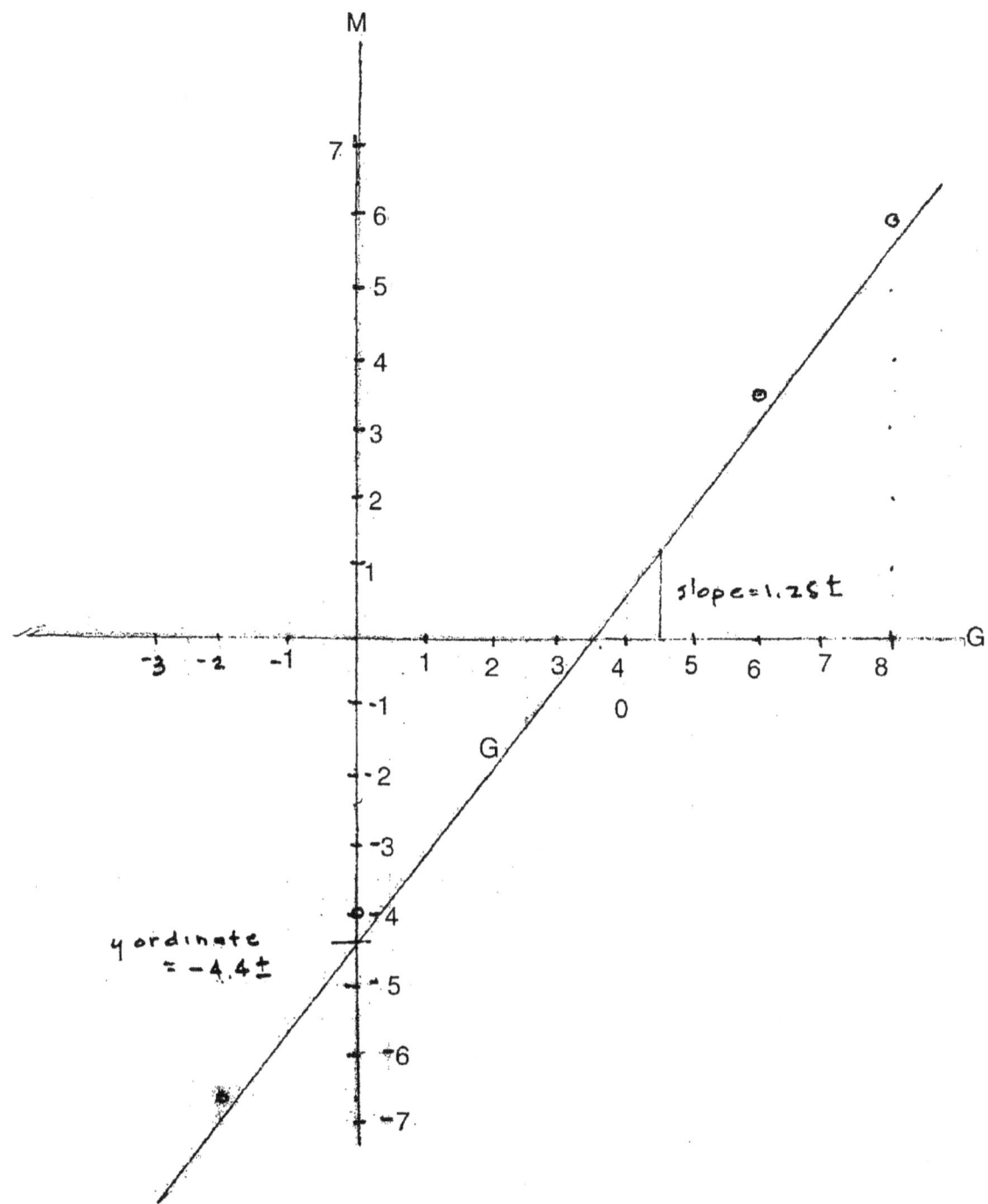

9. CORRECT ANSWER: D
The correlation coefficient, r, is given by:

$$r = \frac{6(\Sigma MG) - (\Sigma M)(\Sigma G)}{\sqrt{[6(\Sigma M^2) - (\Sigma M)^2] \cdot [6(\Sigma G^2) - (\Sigma G)^2]}}$$

$$= \frac{6(75.2) - (18)(-3.6)}{\sqrt{[6(111.06) - (-3.6)^2] \cdot [6(124) - (18)^2]}}$$

$$= 516/\sqrt{(653.4)(420)} \approx +.98$$

10. CORRECT ANSWER: B

The formula is: $n = \hat{p}\hat{q}(\frac{Z_{\alpha/2}}{E})^2$. Since $\hat{p}, \hat{q}$ are unknown, use a value of .5 for each. E = .03 and $Z_{\alpha/2} = Z_{.025} = 1.96$

Then, $n = (.5)(.5)(\frac{1.96}{.03})^2 = 1067.\overline{1} \approx 1067$

11. CORRECT ANSWER: C
Eliminate choice A. By baking 1 cake, his expected profit = (1)(.20) + (1)(.5) + (1)(.3) = $1. By baking 2 cakes, the expected profit = (-1)(.2) + (2)(.5) + (2)(.3) = $1.40. Finally, baking 3 cakes, the profit = (-3)(.2) + (0)(.5) + (3)(.3) = $0.30. He should bake 2 cakes.

12. CORRECT ANSWER: C
This is a classic Buyes' Theorem application.
Let P = tests positive, C = has cancer, C' = does not have cancer, and N = tests negative. Prob (P|C) = .95, Prob (N|C) = .05, Prob (N|C') = .95, Prob (P|C'). = .05. We seek the value of Prob (C|P). We also know Prob (C) = .005 and Prob (C') = .995.

Now Prob (C P) = $\frac{\text{Prob (C)} \cdot \text{Prob (P/C)}}{\text{Prob(C)} \cdot \text{Prob (P|C)} + \text{Prob (C')} \cdot \text{Prob (P/C')}}$

= (.005)(.95)/[(.005)(.95)+(.995)(.05)] $\approx$ .09

13. CORRECT ANSWER: A
For both plants, the rates of days lost per worker in the four age groups are: 6, 8, 10, and 12, respectively.

14. CORRECT ANSWER: B

Since $\frac{1}{k^2} = .05$, $k = \sqrt{20}$. Now, since $ks/\sqrt{n} = s/2$ in this example, we get $\sqrt{20}./\sqrt{n} = \frac{1}{2}$
(s's cancel). Solving, n = 80.

15. CORRECT ANSWER: B
The probability is given by $(_3C_2)(.70)^2(.30)^1 = .441 \approx .44$

16. **CORRECT ANSWER: D**
    The mean, μ, of this population is $(2+4+8+10)/4 = 6$ and its standard deviation, δ, is given by $\sqrt{[(2-6)^2 + (4-6)^2 + (8-6)^2 + (10-6)^2]/4} = \sqrt{10}$.
    For all samples of size taken from this population, the mean, μ_x, is 6 and the standard deviation, $\delta_x = \sqrt{10}/\sqrt{2} \approx 2.236$ so δ_x^2 (variance) = 5. Then, $\mu_x + \delta_x^2 = 11.0$

17. **CORRECT ANSWER: A**
    The only effect of adding a constant to each of the observations is that the y-intercept a will be altered by that constant.
    The b value of y = a + bx and the correlation coefficient remain the same.

18. **CORRECT ANSWER: B**
    Change 65 and 74 to z scores: 65 becomes $(65-68)/3 = -1$
    and 74 becomes $(74-68)/3 = 2$.
    Prob $(-1<z<2)$ in a Normal Distribution $= .3413 + .4772 =$
    $.8185 \approx 82\%$

19. **CORRECT ANSWER: B**
    The 1-column code would be a number from 0 through 7.
    Suppose 0 = yes, 1 = no. The original 3 columns would read as a triple, such as 101. Simply convert this, using the binary system, to a digit from 0 to 7. In this instance, 101 would be 5.

20. **CORRECT ANSWER: A**
    The Type II error denotes accepting a false hypothesis. By increasing this error, we can reduce the Type I error, which signifies rejecting a true hypothesis.

TEST 2

DIRECTIONS: Each question or incomplete statement is followed by several suggested answers or completions. Select the one that BEST answers the question or completes the statement. *PRINT THE LETTER OF THE CORRECT ANSWER IN THE SPACE AT THE RIGHT.*

1. Which BEST describes the method to use in fitting a curve to the data on the population of New York City for the decades from 1790 through 1970?

    A. Logistic
    B. Straight line
    C. Gompertz curve
    D. Parabola

2. Government statistical work can either be organized into one statistical agency that services all departments or into separate statistical units in each department.
   The MAJOR advantage of a central agency is that

    A. one giant computer can service the data needs of all departments
    B. it is more sensitive and responsive to data needs for policy-making
    C. it overcomes the defects of overproliferation of statistical operations
    D. economies of scale lead to less efficiency and the application of greater expertise

3. In many multi-purpose surveys of the characteristics of individuals, some people refuse to report their wage or income data.
   The BEST way to overcome this deficiency is to

    A. get the respondent to answer by threatening to jail or fine him
    B. impute the missing data by having the computer assign the same data for this report as the next report with identical characteristics on other measured variables
    C. look up his income tax record and use the data from this source
    D. leave the columns blank on the punch card and leave such reports out of wage or income tabulations until later research establishes the clarity of such matters

4. The BEST way in which to derive morbidity statistics for all sickness, major and minor, experienced by a population is to

    A. secure the records of a representative sample of industrial establishments on sickness absenteeism
    B. conduct a study of the illnesses and characteristics of hospital in-patients
    C. conduct a study of visits and consultations in stratified samples of general practitioners
    D. conduct a sample survey of the population, and ask them what sickness they had during the last month

5. The point of intersection of the *less than* and *more than* cumulative frequency curves is always at the

    A. arithmetic mean in a bivariate sample
    B. geometric mean in any sample
    C. harmonic mean in a skewed sample
    D. median, whether the sample is skewed or normal

6. In some ways time series analysis is the least satisfying area of statistical analysis from the theoretical viewpoint.
   This statement refers to the fact that

   A. exact data needed for time series analysis are difficult to obtain
   B. time series computations are complex
   C. time series observations are not random drawings from a population
   D. time series represent bivariate data

7. The use of moving averages on a time series will

   A. eliminate bias
   B. make possible predictions of values beyond the range of the original data
   C. provide a mathematical expression for the underlying curve
   D. reveal the general trend

8. Sequential sampling designs should be used when

   A. a decision must be reached in a specified short time
   B. each observation is expensive to get
   C. many test cases are easily available
   D. uniformity of tests is essential

9. As a statistician with no knowledge of computer technology, you have been assigned to be liaison with the computer division on a mass project.
   Your PRIMARY function should be to

   A. review the programming steps to insure accuracy of the program
   B. indicate to the computer section what the statistical input and desired analytic output will be
   C. follow each important step in the processing of the data
   D. devote your time to setting up the input and leave the form of the output to the computer section

10. In comparing parametric with nonparametric methods, the following statement is TRUE: Nonparametric

    A. methods generally require larger samples at the same level of significance
    B. tests use all the information available in sampled data
    C. methods always require larger samples at the same level of significance
    D. statistics are harder to compute

11. A skin specialist reported that adolescent acne (pimples) are twice as common in females as in males. He based this conclusion on an enumeration of all his patients. This is a FAULTY conclusion because

    A. such a result could have been obtained simply by chance
    B. from a statistical and research design point of view, he did not consider the sampling errors of his study
    C. he would have obtained more representative results if he had sampled his patients in accordance with other outside variables
    D. adolescent girls are more likely than boys to be concerned about their appearance and hence are more apt to visit a skin specialist

12. A community has been making population estimates by the cohort method, utilizing births, deaths, and the school census as a measure of net migration. The results of the census seemed to indicate that the population estimate grossly overstated the population. As a statistician, you have been assigned to look into the apparent discrepancy. You should

    A. recommend that the community pay for a new census because you believe that important population groups in your community were undercounted
    B. state that the census as the official count is right and that the estimates were wrong
    C. make a careful analysis of the differences by age, sex, and race to determine the extent and reasons for the differences in the known elements
    D. declare that the census results are wrong since they disagree with the known data

13. The coding of industry and occupation is one of the more difficult parts of the census of population's coding structure.
    In order to check on the accuracy of this coding, you should

    A. machine edit all coding and not rehire workers with too many errors
    B. sample each coder's work and dismiss those who don't meet standards
    C. check all coding 100 percent, and reassign coders who do not meet quality standards
    D. select a sample of each coder's work and, if quality standards are not met, shift the coder to other work

14. In determining whether a sample could have come from a certain universe, we could use either the X^2 test of goodness of fit or the much simpler

    A. Kolmogorov-Smirnov test
    B. Spearman's rank correlation
    C. Mann-Whitney test
    D. Kruskal-Wallis test

15. The criterion that a point estimator from a sample has the lowest variance among all other point estimators of the population parameter is called

    A. unbiasedness   B. sufficiency
    C. consistency   D. efficiency

16. In stratified sampling, it is desirable that each stratum be

    A. equal in size   B. homoscedastic
    C. heterogeneous   D. homogeneous

17. A basic characteristic that distinguishes an electronic computer (EDP) system from the old punch card system (E.A.M.) is the

    A. use of punched card input
    B. ability to get printed output
    C. use of a programmed sequence of operations
    D. use of numeric codes to represent data

18. A statistician gave a series of multiple regression problems, with a large number of variables, to three different computer centers and received three different sets of equations. This kind of mistake is MOST likely to be caused by

   A. differences in rounding procedures used at the computer centers
   B. mistakes in programming since the programs are not likely to be checked among the installations
   C. differential bugs in compilers of different computers
   D. the fact that computers cannot solve large numbers of simultaneous equations

18.____

19. Of the following, the BEST way to detect partisan treatment of data in a statistical study is to

   A. reject the conclusions stated if you do not agree with them
   B. check the conclusions wherever possible by independent investigation
   C. remember that a statement in print provides no statement of reliability
   D. present contradictory evidence, even if unsubstantiated, and observe the reaction

19.____

20. In a recent study of existing health insurance, a small but significant proportion of respondents reported that they had *loss of income protection* under Blue Shield. This was wrong since Blue Shield does not provide such benefits. This type of response error is

   A. balanced by other types of errors
   B. corrected by taking larger samples
   C. not possible to detect by editing techniques
   D. not taken into account by the sampling error formulas

20.____

KEY (CORRECT ANSWERS)

1.	A	11.	D
2.	C	12.	C
3.	B	13.	D
4.	D	14.	A
5.	D	15.	D
6.	C	16.	D
7.	D	17.	C
8.	B	18.	A
9.	B	19.	B
10.	A	20.	D

SOLUTIONS TO PROBLEMS

1. CORRECT ANSWER: A
   Logistic equations are best used to describe population growth.
   A typical equation is $y = S/[1+Ce^{-skt}]$, where y = population at time t, S = maximum population, K = constant, and C = (s-yo)/yo with yo = initial population.

2. CORRECT ANSWER: C
   By having separate units, there would be a tendency for each unit to perform statistical operations, even unnecessarily. The results of these operations then would be difficult to summarize, lacking a central agency.

3. CORRECT ANSWER: B
   Statisticians need to report all data. If a particular variable (wages, other income) is not available for all respondents, the missing data is best replaced by whatever was reported on the next respondent with identical (or very similar) characteristics.

4. CORRECT ANSWER: D
   By conducting a random sample survey, we get a better picture on various morbidity statistics. This is certainly preferable to going to hospitals or to doctors, since we will probably only get data on major sicknesses.

5. CORRECT ANSWER: D
   The median represents the value where exactly one-half of the distribution lies below it and one-half lies above it. Thus, 50% of the values are less than the median and 50% of the values are more than the median.

6. CORRECT ANSWER: C
   Time series involves observations taken at specific intervals, such as each month or each year. In the theoretical sense, statistical formulas and models are based on randomness of events. This is absent from time series analyses.

7. CORRECT ANSWER: D
   A moving average would detect changes in data, large or small. For example, a 3-month moving average would first take the average values of January, February, and March; then the average of February, March, and April, etc. The change in averages would be revealed, and this would indicate any trend.

8. CORRECT ANSWER: C
   Sequential sampling provides for taking as many samples as necessary in order to reach a decision concerning acceptance or rejection of a product. This is possible when many test cases are available (and cost is not a major issue).

9. CORRECT ANSWER: B
   The computer division will be then able to design its program(s) to function so that the statistician can interpret the resulting output correctly.

10. CORRECT ANSWER: A
Non-parametric methods do not require any assumptions concerning the population from which samples are drawn. Their computations are also generally easier than those for parametric methods. As a result, larger samples are needed to attain the same level of significance when a parametric method is used.

11. CORRECT ANSWER: D
Since the skin specialist would examine considerably more females than males, his conclusion about the frequency of acne in girls vs. boys would be faulty.

12. CORRECT ANSWER: C
The statistician needs to examine specific categories which are readily definable, such as age and sex. The errors in the estimate can then be traced to one or more of these defined categories.

13. CORRECT ANSWER: D
To maximize efficiency and accuracy, assign only the best coders to the coding assignment. The other workers would be better suited to an easier task.

14. CORRECT ANSWER: A
This test converts frequencies (observed) to cumulative frequencies and then cumulative proportions are found. Using cumulative proportions of both observed and expected frequencies, the actual test involves comparing D, which is the <u>largest</u> difference between observed and expected frequencies (cumulative). This test is superior to the X^2 test, when the distribution is not normal.

15. CORRECT ANSWER: D
The efficiency of any statistic is measured by the size of its standard error or variance. Since a point estimator has the lowest variance, when drawn from a sample, it has the highest efficiency in the measurement of the corresponding population parameter.

16. CORRECT ANSWER: D
In stratified sampling, we attempt to provide that various homogeneous subgroups are represented in the sample in accordance with their respective representation in the population.

17. CORRECT ANSWER: C
All computer systems use programmable operations and calculations.

18. CORRECT ANSWER: A
Each computer center's capability to identify the exactness of the regression coefficients will differ slightly due to rounding in the calculations.

19. CORRECT ANSWER: B
Self-explanatory.

20. CORRECT ANSWER: D
In this scenario, the respondents did not understand the meaning of *loss of income protection*. The sampling error formulas cannot detect this mistake.

EXAMINATION SECTION
TEST 1

DIRECTIONS: Each question or incomplete statement is followed by several suggested answers or completions. Select the one that BEST answers the question or completes the statement. *PRINT THE LETTER OF THE CORRECT ANSWER IN THE SPACE AT THE RIGHT.*

Questions 1-4.

DIRECTIONS: Questions 1 through 4 are to be answered on the basis of the following information.

In a day care center of 30 children (20 females and 10 males), 7 boys develop hepatitis A over a 3-week period. During the next 8 weeks, an additional 2 boys and 5 girls develop the infection.

1. The attack rate of hepatitis A in this day care center is _____%.
   A. 20   B. 30   C. 40   D. 46.6   E. 54.5

2. The secondary attack rate of hepatitis A in this day care center is MOST NEARLY _____%.
   A. 20   B. 15   C. 23   D. 27   E. 10

3. The attack rate of hepatitis A for boys in this school is MOST NEARLY _____%.
   A. 16   B. 40   C. 50   D. 60   E. 64

4. The attack rate of hepatitis A for girls is MOST NEARLY _____%.
   A. 21   B. 24   C. 25   D. 27   E. 30

5. The epidemic curve suggests a common source outbreak with
   A. continuing common source outbreak
   B. fecal-oral transmission
   C. secondary airborne transmission
   D. secondary person-to-person transmission
   E. none of the above

6. The _____ rate is determined by the number of deaths caused by a specific disease divided by the number of cases of the disease.
   A. mortality   B. case fatality
   C. attack   D. cause specific death
   E. none of the above

7. Rate is the expression of the probability of occurrence of a particular event in a defined population during a specified period of time.
   The rate calculated for various segments of the population is known as the _____ rate.
   A. specific   B. crude
   C. adjusted   D. variable
   E. none of the above

8. The sources of disease surveillance data include all of the following EXCEPT

   A. individual case reports
   B. emergency room visit records
   C. hospital discharge summaries
   D. death certificates
   E. none of the above

9. All of the following are true about tularemia EXCEPT that it is

   A. a zoonotic disease
   B. more common during the summer months in the western states
   C. more common in winter months in the eastern states
   D. primarily transmitted by the bite of a spider
   E. none of the above

10. Which of the following is NOT among the basic steps in an investigation of an epidemic?

    A. Verification of diagnosis
    B. Establishing the existence of an epidemic
    C. Characterization of the distribution of cases
    D. Formulating a conclusion
    E. All of the above

11. The LAST step in conducting an epidemic investigation is to

    A. develop an hypothesis
    B. test the hypothesis
    C. formulate a conclusion
    D. institute control measures
    E. establish the diagnosis of an epidemic

12. The patients who are infected with an agent but never develop clinical symptoms of the disease are known as _____ carriers.

    A. incubatory   B. subclinical   C. chronic
    D. convalescent   E. clinical

13. All of the following are uses of epidemiology EXCEPT to

    A. identify factors that cause disease
    B. explain how and why diseases and epidemics occur
    C. establish a clinical diagnosis of disease
    D. determine a patient's prognosis
    E. evaluate the effectiveness of health programs

14. The biological traits that determine the occurrence of a disease include all of the following EXCEPT

    A. genetic characteristics   B. diet
    C. race   D. ethnic origin
    E. sex

15. The general factors of resistance in a human host include all of the following EXCEPT

    A. the immune system
    B. intact skin
    C. diarrhea
    D. normal bacterial flora
    E. gastric juices

16. All of the following are examples of direct contact transmission EXCEPT

    A. syphilis
    B. herpes
    C. hepatitis B
    D. sporotrichosis
    E. none of the above

17. The basic aims and specific goals of medical studies and clinical research do NOT include

    A. assessing health status or clinical characteristics
    B. eliminating all carriers of diseases
    C. determining and assessing treatment outcomes
    D. identifying and assessing risk factors
    E. all of the above

18. Incidence and prevalence studies usually concern all of the following EXCEPT

    A. the occurrence of disease
    B. a comparison of outcomes between different treatments
    C. adverse side effects of drugs
    D. the death rate for a certain disease
    E. none of the above

19. A case series report can address almost any clinical issue but it is MOST commonly used to describe

    A. clinical characteristics of a disease
    B. screening test results
    C. treatment outcomes
    D. an unexpected result or event
    E. none of the above

20. A comparison of chemotherapy to chemotherapy plus radiation for laryngeal carcinoma would be an appropriate topic for a(n)

    A. cohort study
    B. case control study
    C. clinical trial
    D. case series report
    E. incidence and prevalence study

21. The sum of all values in a series divided by the actual number of values in the series is known as the

    A. mode
    B. median
    C. geometric mean
    D. arithmetic mean
    E. none of the above

22. The MOST commonly occurring value in a series of values is the 22.____

   A. mode
   B. median
   C. geometric mean
   D. arithmetic mean
   E. none of the above

23. The ratio of the standard deviation of a series to the arithmetic mean of the series is known as the 23.____

   A. range
   B. variance
   C. coefficient of variation
   D. standard deviation
   E. epidemic curve

24. The sum of squared deviations from the mean divided by the number of values in the series minus 1 is called the 24.____

   A. range
   B. variance
   C. standard deviation
   D. coefficient of variation
   E. frequency polygon

25. The _____ is a tool for comparing categories of mutually exclusive discrete data. 25.____

   A. pie chart
   B. Venn diagram
   C. bar diagram
   D. histogram
   E. frequency polygon

KEY (CORRECT ANSWERS)

1.	D	11.	D
2.	C	12.	B
3.	E	13.	D
4.	C	14.	B
5.	D	15.	A
6.	B	16.	E
7.	A	17.	B
8.	E	18.	B
9.	D	19.	A
10.	E	20.	C

21	D
22.	A
23.	C
24.	B
25.	C

TEST 2

DIRECTIONS: Each question or incomplete statement is followed by several suggested answers or completions. Select the one that BEST answers the question or completes the statement. *PRINT THE LETTER OF THE CORRECT ANSWER IN THE SPACE AT THE RIGHT.*

1. A _____ is a special form of the bar diagram used to represent categories of continuous and ordered data.

    A. pie chart
    B. histogram
    C. Venn diagram
    D. cumulative frequency graph
    E. frequency polygon

    1.____

2. A medical student performs venipuncture on 1,000 randomly selected patients and is successful on the first attempt 700 times.
   What is the probability that her next venipuncture will be successful on the first attempt?

    A. 7%   B. 14%   C. 50%   D. 70%   E. 80%

    2.____

3. All of the following are true regarding the standard error of the mean of a sample EXCEPT that it

    A. is an estimate of the standard deviation of the population
    B. is based on a normal distribution
    C. increases as the sample size increases
    D. is used to determine confidence limits
    E. none of the above

    3.____

4. All of the following are characteristics of a confidence interval EXCEPT that it

    A. is based on a critical ratio when the sample is large
    B. gives an indication of the likely magnitude of the true value
    C. gives an indication of the certainty of the point estimate
    D. becomes narrower as the sample size increases
    E. none of the above

    4.____

5. Nonparametric tests can be used to compare two populations with which of the following conditions?

    A. Each population is unimodal
    B. Both populations have equal numbers
    C. Each population is independent
    D. Each population is distributed normally
    E. All of the above

    5.____

6. All of the following vaccines are grown in embryonated chicken eggs EXCEPT

    A. yellow fever   B. measles   C. mumps
    D. rubella   E. influenza

    6.____

55

7. Which of the following vaccines should NOT be given to individuals who live in households with an immuno-compromised host?

    A. Yellow fever
    B. Hepatitis B
    C. Oral polio
    D. Influenza
    E. Diphtheriae

8. A solution of antibodies derived from the serum of animals immunized with a specific antigen is a(n)

    A. immunoglobulin
    B. antitoxin
    C. toxoid
    D. vaccine
    E. none of the above

9. All of the following may be significant sequale of measles infection EXCEPT

    A. pneumonia
    B. encephalitis
    C. congenital birth defects
    D. mental retardation
    E. death

10. All of the following statements about vaccination during pregnancy are true EXCEPT:

    A. Live attenuated viral vaccines should not be given to pregnant women
    B. Pregnant women at substantial risk of exposure may receive a live viral vaccine
    C. There is evidence that inactivated vaccines also pose risks to the fetus
    D. There is no evidence that immunoglobulins pose any risk to the fetus
    E. None of the above

11. None of the following conditions are reasons for delaying or discontinuing routine immunizations EXCEPT

    A. soreness, redness or swelling at the injection site in reaction to previous immunization
    B. a temperature of more than 105F in reaction to previous DTP vaccine
    C. mild diarrheal illness in an otherwise well child
    D. current antimicrobial therapy
    E. breastfeeding

12. Children and infants with any of the following disorders should not receive pertussis vaccine EXCEPT those with

    A. uncontrolled epilepsy
    B. infantile spasms
    C. progressive encephalopathy
    D. developmental delay
    E. none of the above

13. Which of the following groups of patients should NOT receive pneumococcal polysaccharide vaccine?

    A. Elderly, age 65 or older
    B. Immunocompromised
    C. Children age 2 years or older with anatomic or functional asplenia

D. Children age 2 years or older with nephrotic syndrome or CSF leaks
E. Children under 2 years of age

14. All of the following are significant complications of sexually transmitted diseases in women EXCEPT

    A. pelvic inflammatory disease
    B. infertility
    C. teratogenicity
    D. cancer
    E. ectopic pregnancy

15. For primary prevention and maximal safety, a person should

    A. engage in a mutually monogamous relationship
    B. limit the number of sexual partners
    C. inspect and question new partners
    D. avoid sexual practices involving anal or fecal contact
    E. all of the above

16. All of the following are complications caused by untreated syphilis infection EXCEPT

    A. obesity   B. blindness
    C. psychosis   D. cardiovascular disease
    E. none of the above

17. All of the following statements are true regarding syphilis EXCEPT:

    A. The organism cannot enter through intact skin
    B. Everyone is susceptible
    C. There is no natural or acquired immunity
    D. No vaccine is available
    E. Reinfection is rare

18. Which of the following sexually transmitted diseases rank as the number one reported communicable disease in the United States?

    A. Syphilis   B. Gonorrhea   C. AIDS
    D. Chlamydia   E. Hepatitis B

19. Which of the following is believed to be the MOST common sexually transmitted bacterial pathogen in the United States?

    A. Treponema pallidum   B. Chlamydia trachomatis
    C. Nisseriae gonorrhea   D. E. coli
    E. Herpes zoster

20. All of the following are documented modes of transmission for human immunodeficiency virus EXCEPT _____ transmission.

    A. sexual   B. percutaneous exposure
    C. airborne   D. mother to child
    E. none of the above

21. In order to prevent HIV infection, which of the following groups should NOT donate blood?

    A. Any man who has had sexual contact with another man since 1977
    B. Present or past IV drug abusers
    C. Individuals from Central Africa and Haiti
    D. Sexual partners of any of the above groups
    E. All of the above

21.____

22. Chlamydia trachomatis, the causative agent of chlamydia infection, has all of the following characteristics EXCEPT it

    A. grows only intracellularly
    B. contains both DNA and RNA
    C. is a protozoa
    D. divides by binary fission
    E. has cell walls similar to gram-negative bacteriae

22.____

23. All of the following are true regarding the resultant effects of chlamydia trachomatis EXCEPT:

    A. Approximately 50% cases of non-gonococcal urethritis in men
    B. 99% of cases of pelvic inflammatory disease
    C. Mucopurulent cervicitis
    D. Inclusion conjunctivitis in infants born to infected mothers
    E. Acute epididymitis in men

23.____

24. All of the following statements are true regarding hepatitis A infection EXCEPT:

    A. Approximately 70% of Americans are infected by the age of 20
    B. Incidence appears to be declining
    C. Infection is related to age and socioeconomic status
    D. The incubation period is 15-50 days with an average of 28-30 days
    E. Young children are more likely to have subclinical infections

24.____

25. The transmission of hepatitis A virus is facilitated by all of the following EXCEPT

    A. poor personal hygiene
    B. poor sanitation
    C. drinking out of the same cup
    D. eating uncooked or raw food
    E. eating food contaminated by human hands after cooking

25.____

KEY (CORRECT ANSWERS)

1. B
2. D
3. C
4. E
5. E

6. D
7. C
8. B
9. C
10. C

11. B
12. D
13. E
14. C
15. E

16. A
17. E
18. B
19. B
20. C

21. E
22. C
23. B
24. A
25. C

EXAMINATION SECTION
TEST 1

DIRECTIONS: Each question or incomplete statement is followed by several suggested answers or completions. Select the one that BEST answers the question or completes the statement. *PRINT THE LETTER OF THE CORRECT ANSWER IN THE SPACE AT THE RIGHT.*

1. Which of the following factors contributes MOST to infant mortality?

    A. Motor vehicle accidents
    B. Congenital cardiac malformation
    C. Prematurity
    D. Acute renal failure
    E. Pneumonia

2. All of the following statements are true regarding tuberculosis in the United States EXCEPT:

    A. Mortality and morbidity rates increase with age
    B. Mortality rates are higher for males than females
    C. The incidence is much higher among the poor than the rich
    D. In low incidence areas, such as the United States, most tuberculosis is exogenous
    E. In 2015, the reported incidence of clinical disease in the United States was 3.0/100,000 population

3. Tubercle bacilli CANNOT be destroyed by

    A. heat   B. cold
    C. ultraviolet light   D. phenol
    E. tricresol solution

4. The MOST frequent reservoirs for tuberculosis disease are

    A. badgers   B. mosquitoes   C. humans
    D. cats   E. deer

5. The LEADING cause of death for people younger than age 65 in the United States is

    A. heart disease
    B. cerebrovascular disease
    C. chronic obstructive pulmonary disease
    D. diabetes mellitus
    E. chronic liver disease

6. Cooling towers and air conditioning units serve as breeding grounds for

    A. staphylococcus aureus
    B. klebsiella pneumoniae
    C. streptococcus pneumoniae
    D. L. pneumophilia
    E. histoplasma capsulatum

7. Diseases transmitted by mosquitoes, mites, and ticks can be prevented by all of the following precautions EXCEPT

   A. protective clothing
   B. mask and gloves
   C. insect repellents
   D. door and window screens
   E. more than one but not all of the above

8. The PRINCIPAL area of study in injury control is

   A. epidemiology
   B. prevention
   C. treatment
   D. rehabilitation
   E. all of the above

9. Benzene is MOST likely to be associated with _____ cancer.

   A. blood
   B. kidney
   C. liver
   D. brain
   E. bone

10. A _____ test is used when the patient's wishes can be inferred from his or her known religious, ethical, and/or lifestyle beliefs.

    A. subjective
    B. relative
    C. limited objective
    D. pure objective
    E. none of the above

11. It is NOT true that standard deviation

    A. is the positive square root of variance
    B. is the most useful measure of dispersion
    C. standardizes extreme values
    D. decreases when the sample size increases
    E. of a small size in a sample causes the sample mean to be close to each individual value

12. The difference between the highest and lowest values in a series is called the

    A. range
    B. variance
    C. standard deviation
    D. coefficient of variation
    E. none of the above

13. The ratio of the standard deviation of a series to the arithmetic mean of the series is known as the

    A. coefficient of variation
    B. range
    C. variance
    D. frequency
    E. prevalence

14. In a disease which is usually of acute onset, lasts a couple of weeks, and has a case fatality rate of 75 to 85%, the

    A. prevalence is always higher than that of annual incidence
    B. incidence is always higher than the prevalence
    C. prevalence and annual incidence are always equal
    D. mortality rate will be consistently high in all countries where the disease occurs
    E. none of the above

15. A random sample of 20,000 men is screened for a history of excessive sugar consumption and the presence of diabetes.
This is called a _____ study.

   A. prospective
   B. historical
   C. cross-sectional population
   D. retrospective-prospective
   E. case control retrospective

16. Five hundred young adults who are known cocaine users are assembled together with a control group. Recognizable psychotics are excluded, and the remainder are followed for 3 years to see whether any psychoses develop in them.
This is a _____ study.

   A. retrospective
   B. case control retrospective
   C. cross-sectional population
   D. cohort
   E. none of the above

17. The FIRST and most important thing for the epidemiologist to do during the investigation of a patient with a communicable disease is to investigate

   A. the first source of infection
   B. the mode of transmission
   C. how many people have been infected
   D. the accuracy of the diagnosis
   E. preventive control of the disease

18. The single MOST important measure for the prevention of typhoid fever in a community is

   A. a ceftriaxon prophylaxis for all persons who are exposed to the disease
   B. washing hands
   C. immunization of the high risk population
   D. hospitalization and treatment of all known carriers
   E. water purification

19. Diseases more likely to occur in women than in men include all of the following EXCEPT

   A. Raynaud's disease
   B. sarcoidosis
   C. gout
   D. systemic lupus erythematosus
   E. secondary hypothyroidism

20. Over the past 50 years, which of the following chronic conditions has experienced the greatest decline in mortality rate?

   A. Heart disease
   B. Stroke
   C. Cancer
   D. Pneumonia
   E. Influenza

21. The population having the HIGHEST frequency of thalassemia is the

   A. Jews
   B. Italians
   C. Chinese
   D. Japanese
   E. Americans

22. Over the past ten years, the majority of individuals who were initially diagnosed with diabetes mellitus were in what age group?

   A. 18-29
   B. 30-39
   C. 50-59
   D. 70-79
   E. 80-89

23. Of the following, the disease LARGELY confined to people born in temperate climate zones and manifested in early adult life is

   A. diabetes
   B. multiple sclerosis
   C. thalassemia
   D. hypertension
   E. prostate cancer

24. Hepatitis A has the highest incidence rate in individuals in which age group?

   A. 0-9
   B. 10-19
   C. 20-29
   D. 30-39
   E. 50-59

25. Recurrent episodes of low grade fever and arthralgia FREQUENTLY affect workers in

   A. slaughter houses
   B. cotton mills
   C. coal mines
   D. hospital laboratories
   E. none of the above

KEY (CORRECT ANSWERS)

1. C		11. C	
2. D		12. A	
3. B		13. A	
4. C		14. B	
5. A		15. C	
6. D		16. D	
7. B		17. D	
8. E		18. E	
9. A		19. C	
10. C		20. B	

21. B
22. C
23. B
24. C
25. A

TEST 2

DIRECTIONS: Each question or incomplete statement is followed by several suggested answers or completions. Select the one that BEST answers the question or completes the statement. *PRINT THE LETTER OF THE CORRECT ANSWER IN THE SPACE AT THE RIGHT.*

1. Risk factors for malignancies of the liver and intra-hepatic biliary tract may include all of the following EXCEPT   1____

    A. alpha-1 antitrypsin deficiency
    B. aflatoxin
    C. gentamicin
    D. alcohol
    E. steroids

2. The parasite associated with an increased risk for developing carcinoma of the biliary tree is   2____

    A. ascaris lumbricoides
    B. balantidium coli
    C. cryptoporidium
    D. colonorchis sinensis
    E. enterobias vermicular is

3. Of the following, the immunization that should NOT be given to an individual who has received immune globulin within the previous 3 months is   3____

    A. IPV
    B. DTP
    C. MMR
    D. HBIG
    E. none of the above

4. Which of the following is the LEADING cause of maternal death among pregnancies with abortive outcomes?   4____

    A. Rubella
    B. Ectopic pregnancy
    C. Teratoma
    D. Defective germ cell
    E. Herpes simplex II

5. All of the following are leading causes of maternal mortality in the United States EXCEPT   5____

    A. anesthesia complication
    B. embolism
    C. hypertensive disease of pregnancy
    D. hemorrhage
    E. maternal age between 20 and 30

6. _____ is NOT a reportable disease.   6____

    A. Pulmonary tuberculosis
    B. Mumps
    C. Measles
    D. Choriomeningitis
    E. Meningococcal sepsis

7. The scientific field dealing with the collection, classification, description, analysis, interpretation, and presentation of data is called   7____

    A. distributions
    B. statistics
    C. standard deviation
    D. median
    E. cohort study

8. What type of treatment regimen should be administered to an infant born to a mother with active gonorrhea?

    A. Single IM dose of ceftriaxone
    B. Single oral dose of azithromycin
    C. Dual therapy of ceftriaxone and azithromycin
    D. Dual therapy of ceftriaxone and spectinomycin
    E. None of the above

9. A precaution necessary for children in day care who have pneumococcal disease is _____ isolation.

    A. strict   B. contact   C. enteric
    D. respiratory   E. none of the above

10. Children who have ever had a life-threatening allergic reaction to _____ should not get the polio vaccine.

    A. gluten   B. peanuts   C. eggs
    D. antibiotics   E. pollen

11. Stillbirths or perinatal death is a result of _____ % of pregnancies in women with untreated early syphilis.

    A. 5   B. 10   C. 25   D. 40   E. 80

12. Strongyloidiasis is endemic in the tropics and subtropics, including the southern and southwestern United States. The single MOST important control measure is

    A. purification of water
    B. food cooked at a higher temperature
    C. sanitary disposal measure for human waste
    D. mass vaccination of exposed population
    E. detection and treatment of all infected persons

13. In a large population, the mode of transmission MOST difficult to prevent is _____ spread.

    A. vector   B. person to person
    C. airborne   D. droplet
    E. none of the above

14. Of the following, the factor contributing the MOST to infant mortality is

    A. seizures   B. prematurity   C. hypothyroidism
    D. congenital heart disease E. birth trauma

15. Point prevalence studies tend to have an over-representation of

    A. chronic cases   B. fatal cases   C. short-term cases
    D. healthy persons   E. all of the above

16. The PRIMARY function of the federal government in the Medicaid program is to

    A. set standards
    B. provide services in their own institutions *only*
    C. investigate *only* services rendered
    D. pay for services
    E. pay for nursing care *only*

Questions 17-21.

DIRECTIONS: In Questions 17 through 21, match the numbered description with the appropriate lettered term listed in Column I. Place the letter of the correct answer in the space at the right.

<u>COLUMN I</u>
A. Sensitivity
B. Specificity
C. Screening
D. Median
E. Mode

17. The MOST commonly occurring value in a series of values   17____

18. The initial examination of an individual whose disease is not yet under medical care   18____

19. May be calculated in an ongoing longevity study   19____

20. The ability of a screening test to identify correctly those individuals who truly have the disease   20____

21. The ability of a test to identify correctly those individuals who truly do not have the disease   21____

Questions 22-25.

DIRECTIONS: In Questions 22 through 25, match the numbered definition with the appropriate lettered term listed in Column I. Place the letter of the correct answer in the space at the right.

<u>COLUMN I</u>
A. Efficiency
B. Validity
C. Reliability
D. Bias
E. Causality

22. The extent to which a test provides the same result on the same subject on two or more occasions   22____

23. The extent to which the results of a test agree with the results of another test that is accepted as more accurate or closer to the truth   23____

24. A systematic error that is unintentionally made   24____

25. Denotes direct effect   25____

KEY (CORRECT ANSWERS)

1.	C	11.	D
2.	D	12.	C
3.	C	13.	C
4.	B	14.	B
5.	E	15.	C
6.	D	16.	D
7.	B	17.	E
8.	C	18.	C
9.	E	19.	D
10.	D	20.	A

21. B
22. C
23. B
24. D
25. E

EXAMINATION SECTION
TEST 1

DIRECTIONS: Each question or incomplete statement is followed by several suggested answers or completions. Select the one that BEST answers the question or completes the statement. *PRINT THE LETTER OF THE CORRECT ANSWER IN THE SPACE AT THE RIGHT.*

1. The MOST common cause of death before age 65 is

   A. cerebrovascular disease
   B. malignant neoplasm
   C. heart disease
   D. diabetes mellitus
   E. liver cirrhosis

   1.____

2. Of the following, the disease NOT transmitted by mosquitoes is

   A. dengue fever
   B. lymphocytic choriomeningitis
   C. western equine encephalitis
   D. St. Louis encephalitis
   E. yellow fever

   2.____

3. The single MOST effective measure to prevent hookworm infection is

   A. washing hands
   B. washing clothes daily
   C. cooking food at high temperatures
   D. wearing shoes
   E. none of the above

   3.____

4. Transmission of tuberculosis in the United States occurs MOST often by

   A. fomites
   B. blood transfusion
   C. inhalation of droplet
   D. transplacentally
   E. milk

   4.____

5. The second MOST common cause of death in the United States is

   A. accident
   B. cancer
   C. cerebrovascular disease
   D. heart disease
   E. AIDS

   5.____

6. All of the following bacteria are spread through fecal-oral transmission EXCEPT

   A. haemophilus influenza type B
   B. campylobacter
   C. escherichia coli
   D. salmonella
   E. shigella

   6.____

7. Routine immunization is particularly important for children in day care because pre-school-aged children currently have the highest age specific incidence of all of the following EXCEPT

   A. H-influenzae type B
   B. neisseria meningitis
   C. measles
   D. rubella
   E. pertussis

   7.____

8. Hand washing and masks are necessary for physical contact with all of the following patients EXCEPT

   A. lassa fever
   B. diphtheria
   C. coxsackie virus disease
   D. varicella
   E. plaque

9. Control measures for prevention of tick-borne infections include all of the following EXCEPT:

   A. Tick-infested area should be avoided whenever possible.
   B. If a tick-infested area is entered, protective clothing that covers the arms, legs, and other exposed area should be worn.
   C. Tick/insect repellent should be applied to the skin.
   D. Ticks should be removed promptly.
   E. Daily inspection of pets and removal of ticks is not indicated.

10. The PRINCIPAL reservoir of giardia lamblia infection is

    A. humans
    B. mosquitoes
    C. rodents
    D. sandflies
    E. cats

11. Most community-wide epidemics of giardia lamblia infection result from

    A. inhalation of droplets
    B. eating infected meats
    C. eating contaminated eggs
    D. drinking contaminated water
    E. blood transfusions

12. Epidemics of giardia lamblia occurring in day care centers are USUALLY caused by

    A. inhalation of droplets
    B. person-to-person contact
    C. fecal and oral contact
    D. eating contaminated food
    E. all of the above

13. Measures of the proportion of the population exhibiting a phenomenon at a particular time is called the

    A. incidence
    B. prevalence
    C. prospective study
    D. cohort study
    E. all of the above

14. The occurrence of an event or characteristic over a period of time is called

    A. incidence
    B. prevalence
    C. specificity
    D. case control study
    E. cohort study

15. All of the following are live attenuated viral vaccines EXCEPT

    A. measles
    B. mumps
    C. rubella
    D. rabies
    E. yellow fever

16. Chlorinating air-cooling towers can prevent

    A. scarlet fever
    B. impetigo
    C. typhoid fever
    D. mycobacterium tuberculosis
    E. legionnaire's disease

17. Eliminating the disease causing agent may be done by all of the following methods EXCEPT

    A. chemotherapeutic
    B. cooling
    C. heating
    D. chlorinating
    E. disinfecting

18. Which of the following medications is used to eliminate pharyngeal carriage of neisseria meningitidis?

    A. Penicillin
    B. Rifampin
    C. Isoniazid
    D. Erythromycin
    E. Gentamicin

19. Post-exposure prophylaxis is recommended for rabies after the bite of all of the following animals EXCEPT

    A. chipmunks
    B. skunks
    C. raccoons
    D. bats
    E. foxes

20. To destroy the spores of clostridium botulinum, canning requires a temperature of AT LEAST _____ °C.

    A. 40   B. 60   C. 80   D. 100   E. 120

21. All of the following are killed or fractionated vaccines EXCEPT

    A. hepatitis B
    B. yellow fever
    C. H-influenza type B
    D. pneumococcus
    E. rabies

22. Of the following, the disease NOT spreadly by food is

    A. typhoid fever
    B. shigellosis
    C. typhus
    D. cholera
    E. legionellosis

23. In the United States, the HIGHEST attack rate of sheigella infection occurs in children between _____ of age.

    A. 1 to 6 months
    B. 6 months to 1 year
    C. 1 to 4 years
    D. 6 to 10 years
    E. 10 to 15 years

24. Risk factors for cholera include all of the following EXCEPT

    A. occupational exposure
    B. lower socioeconomic
    C. unsanitary condition
    D. high socioeconomic
    E. high population density in low income areas

25. The MOST common cause of traveler's diarrhea is 25._____
    A. escherichia coli
    B. shigella
    C. salmonella
    D. cholera
    E. campalobacter

KEY (CORRECT ANSWERS)

1. C
2. B
3. D
4. C
5. B

6. A
7. B
8. C
9. E
10. A

11. D
12. B
13. B
14. A
15. D

16. E
17. B
18. B
19. A
20. E

21. B
22. C
23. C
24. D
25. A

TEST 2

DIRECTIONS: Each question or incomplete statement is followed by several suggested answers or completions. Select the one that BEST answers the question or completes the statement. *PRINT THE LETTER OF THE CORRECT ANSWER IN THE SPACE AT THE RIGHT.*

1. The increased prevalence of entamoeba histolytica infection results from

   A. lower socioeconomic status in endemic area
   B. institutionalized (especially mentally retarded) population
   C. immigrants from endemic area
   D. promiscuous homosexual men
   E. all of the above

   1.____

2. The MOST common infection acquired in the hospital is _____ infection.

   A. surgical wound
   B. lower respiratory tract
   C. urinary tract
   D. bloodstream
   E. gastrointestinal

   2.____

3. The etiologic agent of Rocky Mountain spotted fever is

   A. rickettsia prowazekii
   B. rickettsia rickettsii
   C. rickettsia akari
   D. coxiella burnetii
   E. rochalimaena quintana

   3.____

4. The annual death rate for injuries per 100,000 in both sexes is HIGHEST in those _____ years of age.

   A. 1 to 10
   B. 10 to 20
   C. 30 to 40
   D. 50 to 60
   E. 80 to 90

   4.____

5. The death rate per 100,000 population due to motor vehicle accident is HIGHEST among

   A. whites
   B. blacks
   C. Asians
   D. native Americans
   E. Spanish surnamed

   5.____

6. Among the following, the HIGHEST rate of homicide occurs in

   A. whites
   B. blacks
   C. native Americans
   D. Asians
   E. Spanish surnamed

   6.____

7. All of the following are true statements regarding coronary heart disease EXCEPT:

   A. About 4.6 million Americans have coronary heart disease.
   B. Men have a greater risk of MI and sudden death.
   C. Women have a greater risk of angina pectoris.
   D. 25% of coronary heart disease death occurs in individuals under the age of 65 years.
   E. White women have a greater risk of MI and sudden death.

   7.____

8. Major risk factors for coronary heart disease include all of the following EXCEPT

    A. smoking
    B. elevated blood pressure
    C. obesity
    D. high level of serum cholesterol
    E. family history of coronary heart disease

9. The MOST common cancer in American men is

    A. stomach   B. lung   C. leukemia
    D. prostate   E. skin

10. The HIGHEST incidence of prostate cancer occurs in _____ Americans.

    A. white   B. black   C. Chinese
    D. Asian   E. Spanish

11. All of the following are risk factors for cervical cancer EXCEPT

    A. smoking
    B. low socioeconomic condition
    C. first coital experience after age 20
    D. multiple sexual partners
    E. contracting a sexually transmitted disease

12. All of the following are independent adverse prognostic factors for lung cancer EXCEPT

    A. female sex
    B. short duration of symptom
    C. small cell histology
    D. metastatic disease at time of diagnosis
    E. persistently elevated CEA

13. Assuming vaccines with 80% efficacy were available in limited quantity, which vaccine among the following should be given to a military recruit?

    A. Polio   B. Pseudomonas
    C. Meningococcus   D. Influenza
    E. None of the above

14. Among the following, the vaccine which should be administered to children with sickle cell disease is

    A. influenza   B. meningococcus
    C. pseudomonas   D. pneumococcal
    E. yellow fever

15. All of the following are correct statements concerning gastric carcinoma in the United States EXCEPT:

    A. The risk for males is 2.2 times greater than for females.
    B. The incidence is increased.
    C. The risk is higher in persons with pernicious anemia than for the general population.

D. City dwellers have an increased risk of stomach cancer.
E. Workers with high levels of exposure to nickle and rubber are at increased risk.

16. During the first year of life, a condition that can be detected by screening is

    A. hypothyroidism
    B. RH incompatibility
    C. phenylketonuria
    D. congenital dislocation of the hip
    E. all of the above

17. The major reservoir of the spread of tuberculosis within a hospital is through

    A. patients   B. custodial staff
    C. doctors   D. nursing staff
    E. undiagnosed cases

18. All of the following statements are true regarding tuberculosis EXCEPT:

    A. Droplet nuclei are the major vehicle for the spread of tuberculosis infection.
    B. The highest incidence is among white Americans.
    C. There is a higher incidence of tuberculosis in prison than in the general population.
    D. HIV infection is a significant independent risk factor for the development of tuberculosis.
    E. A single tubercle bacillus, once having gained access to the terminal air spaces, could establish infection.

19. The human papiloma virus is associated with

    A. kaposi sarcoma
    B. hepatoma
    C. cervical neoplasia
    D. nasopharyngeal carcinoma
    E. none of the above

20. General recommendations for prevention of sexually transmitted diseases include all of the following EXCEPT

    A. contact tracing   B. disease reporting
    C. barrier methods   D. prophylactic antibiotic use
    E. patient education

21. Syphilis remains an important sexually transmitted disease because of all of the following EXCEPT its

    A. public health heritage
    B. effect on perinatal morbidity and mortality
    C. association with HIV transmission
    D. escalating rate among black teenagers
    E. inability to be prevented

22. Which of the following statements about homicide is NOT true? Approximately

   A. forty percent are committed by friends and acquaintances
   B. twenty percent is committed by spouse
   C. fifteen percent is committed by a member of the victim's family
   D. fifteen percent is committed by strangers
   E. fifteen percent are labeled *relationship unknown*

22.____

23. Conditions for which screening has proven cost-effective include

   A. phenylketonuria
   B. iron deficiency anemia
   C. lead poisoning
   D. tuberculosis
   E. all of the above

23.____

24. Suicide is MOST common among

   A. whites
   B. blacks
   C. hispanics
   D. Asians
   E. none of the above

24.____

25. The MOST frequenty used method of suicide is

   A. hanging
   B. poisoning by gases
   C. firearms
   D. drug overdose
   E. drowning

25.____

KEY (CORRECT ANSWERS)

1. E
2. C
3. B
4. E
5. D

6. B
7. E
8. C
9. D
10. B

11. C
12. A
13. C
14. D
15. B

16. E
17. E
18. B
19. C
20. D

21. E
22. B
23. E
24. A
25. C

EXAMINATION SECTION
TEST 1

DIRECTIONS: Each question or incomplete statement is followed by several suggested answers or completions. Select the one that BEST answers the question or completes the statement. *PRINT THE LETTER OF THE CORRECT ANSWER IN THE SPACE AT THE RIGHT.*

1. A PPD reaction of greater than or equal to 5 mm induration is considered positive in all of the following individuals EXCEPT

    A. persons with HIV infection
    B. IV drug abusers who are HIV antibody negative
    C. close recent contacts of an infectious tuberculosis case
    D. persons with a chest radiograph consistent with old, healed tuberculosis
    E. persons with HIV infection or with risk factors for HIV infection who have an unknown IV antibody status

2. All of the following are true about tuberculosis EXCEPT:

    A. The causative agent is M. tuberculosis var. hominis
    B. It is more likely to occur in older individuals (more than 45 years of age)
    C. It is more common in non-whites than in whites
    D. It is more common in men than in women
    E. About 90% of cases in the United States represent new infections

3. The groups that should benefit from preventive therapy for tuberculosis include all of the following EXCEPT

    A. individuals whose skin test has converted from negative to positive in the previous 2 years
    B. individuals with positive mantoux test and with HIV infection
    C. tuberculin-negative IV drug abusers
    D. tuberculin-positive individuals under 35 years of age
    E. individuals with immunosuppressive therapy who are tuberculin positive

4. INH prophylaxis should not be used in any of the following EXCEPT in

    A. the presence of clinical disease
    B. a pregnant woman who has recently converted to tuberculin positive
    C. patients with unstable hepatic function
    D. individuals who were previously adequately treated
    E. individuals with a previous adverse reaction to INH

5. What is the MOST common cause of bacterial meningitis in children under age 5?

    A. Streptococcus pneumoniae
    B. H. influenza
    C. N. meningitidis
    D. E. coli
    E. Staphylococcus aureus

6. All of the following are true about H. influenza infection EXCEPT:

    A. Peak incidence is from age 3 months to 2 years
    B. The mortality rate is about 5%
    C. Secondary spread to day care contacts under 4 years of age is rare
    D. About two-thirds of the cases occur in children under 15 months of age
    E. None of the above

7. All of the following statements are true about hemophilus influenza type B infection EXCEPT:

    A. Rifampin is the drug of choice for chemoprophylaxis
    B. Rifampin may be given to pregnant women
    C. The disease is more common in native and black Americans
    D. Humans are the reservoir of infections
    E. None of the above

8. All of the following statements are true about meningococcal meningitis EXCEPT:

    A. It is the second most common cause of bacterial meningitis in the United States
    B. The peak incidence is around age 6-12 months
    C. Most cases occur in late winter and early spring
    D. The portal of entry is not the nasopharynx
    E. It is more likely to occur in newly aggregated young adults who are living in institutions and barracks

9. Antimicrobial chemoprophylaxis is the chief preventive measure in sporadic cases of meningococcal meningitis and should be offered to

    A. household contacts
    B. day care center contacts
    C. medical personnel who resuscitated, intubated or suctioned the patient before antibiotics were instituted
    D. all patients who were treated for meningococcal disease before discharge from the hospital
    E. all of the above

10. What is the MOST common cause of bacterial meningitis in children under 5 years of age?

    A. Streptococcus pneumoniae
    B. Nisseriae meningitidis
    C. Listeria monocytogenes
    D. Group B streptococcus
    E. Hemophilus influenza type B

11. All of the following are true about coronary heart disease EXCEPT:

    A. It is the leading cause of death in the United States
    B. About 4.6 million Americans have coronary heart disease
    C. It is most common in white men
    D. Women have a greater risk of myocardial infarction and sudden death
    E. Women have a greater risk of angina pectoris

12. According to the National Cholesterol Education Panel, which of the following is NOT a major risk factor for coronary artery disease?

    A. Women 55 years and older
    B. Hypertension
    C. Individuals with diabetes mellitus
    D. High density lipoprotein (HDL) less than 35 mg/dl
    E. Obesity

13. The number one cause of cancer death in the United States is _____ cancer.

    A. lung   B. breast   C. colorectal
    D. cervical   E. prostatic

14. The MOST common cancer in American men is _____ cancer.

    A. lung   B. breast   C. prostate
    D. colon   E. esophageal

15. All of the following are risk factors for women to develop breast cancer EXCEPT

    A. exposure to ionizing radiation
    B. becoming pregnant for the first time after age 30
    C. mother and sisters having breast cancer
    D. high socioeconomic status
    E. late menarchae

16. Cervical cancer is one of the leading causes of death among women. Of the following, which is NOT a risk factor for developing cervical cancer?

    A. Multiple sexual partners
    B. First coitus before age 20
    C. Low socioeconomic status
    D. Oral contraceptive use
    E. Partners of uncircumcised men

17. Population subgroups at INCREASED risk of developing anemia include

    A. women   B. elderly men
    C. children   D. blacks
    E. all of the above

18. Uncontrolled hypertensive disease increases the risk of developing all of the following disorders EXCEPT

    A. coronary heart disease   B. diabetes mellitus
    C. renal disease   D. cerebrovascular disease
    E. none of the above

19. All of the following statements are true regarding chronic obstructive pulmonary disease (COPD) EXCEPT:

    A. Men are at higher risk than women
    B. An estimated 16 million Americans have chronic bronchitis, asthma or emphysema
    C. The risk is related to the duration of smoking only

D. The risk is related to the number of cigarettes smoked daily and to the duration of smoking
E. Offspring of affected individuals are at higher risk

20. Which of the following statements is TRUE regarding diabetes in the United States?   20.____

    A. It accounts for 5% of all deaths.
    B. Its prevalence is estimated at 15%.
    C. 80% of all diabetics have the non-insulin dependent type.
    D. It is the leading cause of blindness.
    E. Men are at greater risk than women.

21. People with increased risk for suicide include all of the following EXCEPT   21.____

    A. drug users   B. married individuals
    C. teenagers   D. chronically depressed
    E. homosexuals

22. Conditions associated with an increased risk for suicide include all of the following EXCEPT   22.____

    A. unemployed
    B. seriously physically ill or handicapped
    C. chronically mentally ill
    D. substance abusers
    E. none of the above

23. The leading cause of death among black men aged 15-24 years is   23.____

    A. automobile accidents   B. homicide
    C. cancer   D. drug abuse
    E. AIDS

24. All of the following are true regarding pernicious anemia EXCEPT: 24.____

    A. It primarily affects individuals over the age of 30
    B. The incidence increases with age
    C. It is more common in Asians and blacks
    D. It is caused by a vitamin B_{12} deficiency
    E. None of the above

25. Which of the following groups of individuals have a high risk of injuries?   25.____

    A. Factory workers
    B. Alcoholics
    C. Individuals with osteoporosis
    D. Homeless
    E. All of the above

KEY (CORRECT ANSWERS)

1.	B	11.	D
2.	E	12.	D
3.	C	13.	A
4.	B	14.	C
5.	B	15.	E
6.	C	16.	C
7.	B	17.	E
8.	D	18.	B
9.	E	19.	C
10.	E	20.	D

21. B
22. E
23. B
24. C
25. E

TEST 2

DIRECTIONS: Each question or incomplete statement is followed by several suggested answers or completions. Select the one that BEST answers the question or completes the statement. *PRINT THE LETTER OF THE CORRECT ANSWER IN THE SPACE AT THE RIGHT.*

1. Which of the following factors does NOT increase a woman's risk of an ectopic pregnancy?

    A. Progestin exposure
    B. Pelvic inflammatory disease
    C. Smoking
    D. Use of alcohol
    E. Infertility

    1._____

2. Breastfeeding usually enhances all of the following EXCEPT

    A. bonding between mother and infant
    B. infant nutrition
    C. immune defenses
    D. antibody response against HIV virus
    E. return of uterus to prepregnant size

    2._____

3. Which of the following is NOT a leading cause of maternal mortality in the United States?

    A. Hypertensive disease of pregnancy
    B. Cardiovascular accidents
    C. Miscarriage
    D. Anesthesia complications
    E. All of the above

    3._____

4. A well-woman prenatal visit should include all of the following EXCEPT a(n)

    A. weight check
    B. blood pressure check
    C. electronic fetal monitoring
    D. pap smear
    E. urine analysis

    4._____

5. All of the following substances or conditions are harmful to the fetus during gestation EXCEPT

    A. tetracycline   B. alcohol   C. herpes
    D. rubella   E. thalidomide

    5._____

6. The use of an intrauterine device (IUD) has been associated with increased risk of

    A. ectopic pregnancy
    B. pelvic inflammatory disease
    C. infertility
    D. infections
    E. all of the above

    6._____

82

7. The number of deaths among infants less than 28 days old per 1,000 live births is called the _____ mortality rate.

   A. neonatal
   B. post-neonatal
   C. fetal
   D. perinatal
   E. none of the above

8. All of the following are causes of postneonatal mortality EXCEPT

   A. lower respiratory tract infections
   B. intrauterine growth retardation
   C. congenital anomalies
   D. sudden infant death syndrome
   E. injuries, e.g., motor vehicle accidents

9. All of the following are important factors in the identification of high risk parents and in the management and prevention of infant health problems EXCEPT

   A. intrauterine infections
   B. pre-existing maternal illnesses
   C. paternal age
   D. maternal history of reproductive problems
   E. family history of hereditary disease

10. Screening for which of the following conditions has been proven to be cost effective?

    A. Phenylketonuria
    B. Congenital hypothyroidism
    C. Lead poisoning
    D. Tuberculosis
    E. All of the above

11. Children _____ are more likely to receive inadequate well-child care.

    A. with chronic health problems
    B. on medicaid
    C. of mothers who started receiving prenatal care late in the second or third trimester
    D. of parents whose jobs do not provide health insurance
    E. all of the above

12. Injuries are classified by the intent or purposefulness of occurrence. All of the following are classified as intentional injuries EXCEPT

    A. child abuse
    B. motor vehicle mishaps
    C. sexual assault
    D. domestic violence
    E. abuse of the elderly

13. Schizophrenia is a disorder, or group of disorders, with a variety of symptoms that include

    A. delusions
    B. hallucinations
    C. agitation
    D. apathy
    E. all of the above

14. All of the following are true about the incidence and prevalence of bipolar disorder EXCEPT:

A. Approximately 4-5% of the population is at risk
B. More women are admitted to the hospital with the diagnosis of bipolar disorder than men
C. The manic form occurs primarily in younger individuals
D. Bipolar patients are more likely to be unmarried
E. The depressive form occurs primarily in older individuals

15. In schizophrenia, there is an increased risk for all of the following EXCEPT

   A. malabsorption syndrome
   B. arteriosclerotic heart disease
   C. hypothyroidism
   D. cancer
   E. none of the above

16. A 6-month-old Jewish infant has a history of seizures, progressive blindness, deafness, and paralysis with an exaggerated startle response to sound.
    The MOST likely diagnosis is

   A. phenylketonuria   B. Gaucher's disease
   C. Tay Sachs disease   D. homocystinuria
   E. maple syrup disease

17. The MOST common inborn error of amino acid metabolism results in

   A. phenylketonuria   B. maple syrup disease
   C. homocystinuria   D. albinism
   E. Gaucher's disease

18. The MOST common lysosomal storage disease is

   A. Niemann-Pick disease   B. Gaucher's disease
   C. Tay Sachs disease   D. homocystinuria
   E. none of the above

19. All of the following are true about spina bifida EXCEPT:

   A. The most common type is spina bifida occulta
   B. The least severe form is myelocoele
   C. Encephalocoele is the rarest type
   D. The most common site affected is lower back
   E. The familial risk of recurrence is approximately 5%

Questions 20-25.

DIRECTIONS: For each metal listed in Questions 20 through 25, select the condition in the column below that is MOST likely to result from chronic exposure to it.

20. Lead   A. Osteomalacia-like disease
21. Arsenic   B. Granulomas of skin and lungs
22. Cadmium   C. Abnormal sperms
23. Mercury   D. Nasal septal ulceration
24. Beryllium   E. Visual field abnormalities
25. Zinc   F. Metal fume fever

KEY (CORRECT ANSWERS)

1.	D		11.	E
2.	D		12.	B
3.	C		13.	E
4.	C		14.	D
5.	C		15.	D
6.	E		16.	C
7.	A		17.	A
8.	B		18.	C
9.	C		19.	B
10.	E		20.	C

21. D
22. A
23. E
24. B
25. F

EXAMINATION SECTION
TEST 1

DIRECTIONS: Each question or incomplete statement is followed by several suggested answers or completions. Select the one that BEST answers the question or completes the statement. *PRINT THE LETTER OF THE CORRECT ANSWER IN THE SPACE AT THE RIGHT.*

1. The _____ virus MOST likely causes AIDS.

    A. picorna
    B. retro
    C. rhino
    D. para influenza
    E. respiratory syncytial

2. Which of the following is MOST likely impaired in patients with HIV?

    A. Complement
    B. T-cell mediated immunity
    C. B-cell mediated immunity
    D. Basophil
    E. Eosinophil

3. Common modes of transmission of the HIV virus is through

    A. contaminated needles
    B. transfusion of blood or blood products
    C. intimate sexual contact
    D. infected mother to fetus
    E. all of the above

4. Which of the following vaccines should NOT be given to a child with HIV?

    A. OPV
    B. Hemophilus type B
    C. MMR
    D. DTP
    E. Pneumococcal

5. All of the following are true statements regarding confidentiality about AIDS EXCEPT:

    A. No one besides the child's physician has an absolute need to know the child's primary diagnosis.
    B. The family has the right to inform the school.
    C. The teacher has the right to inform other students.
    D. Persons involved in the care and education of an infected student must respect the student's right to privacy.
    E. Confidential records should be maintained.

6. Adults with HIV infection working in a day care center or a school

    A. should consult their physician regarding the safety of their continuing to work
    B. are not immuno-compromised if they have symptomatic HIV infection
    C. asymptomatic HIV infected adult may care for children in school with skin lesions and open wounds
    D. are at low risk from infectious diseases of children
    E. none of the above

7. A 16-year-old male comes to you for advice about how to protect himself from HIV infection.
   You should tell him all of the following EXCEPT:

   A. Don't inject drugs.
   B. Don't share needles with other people.
   C. Don't have multiple sexual partners.
   D. Use contraceptive pills for sexual contact.
   E. Use condoms for sexual contacts.

8. Among the following, the MOST common cause of focal intracerebral lesions in patients with AIDS is

   A. cryptococcoma
   B. toxoplasmosis
   C. kaposi's sarcoma
   D. mycobacterium tuberculosis abscess
   E. lymphoma

9. A risk factor associated with heterosexual transmission of AIDS includes

   A. lack of condom
   B. anal intercourse
   C. sex during menses
   D. number of sexual contacts
   E. all of the above

10. The MOST frequent malignancy seen in homosexual men with HIV is

    A. kaposi sarcoma
    B. oat cell carcinoma of lung
    C. medullary carcinoma of thyroid
    D. seminoma
    E. infiltrating carcinoma of breast

11. Mother to infant transmission of HIV occurs in approximately _____% of the infants born to seropositive mothers.

    A. 2-5   B. 8-12   C. 15-30   D. 50   E. 75

12. The MOST frequent neurologic clinical manifestation of primary HIV-1 infection includes

    A. peripheral neuropathy
    B. meningoencephalitis
    C. retro orbital pain
    D. cognitive/affective impairment
    E. all of the above

13. The MOST likely dermatologic manifestation of primary HIV-1 infection includes

    A. diffuse urticaria   B. desquamation
    C. alopecia   D. mucocutaneous ulceration
    E. all of the above

14. Recommendation for the early stages of disease due to HIV infection include

    A. update immunization
    B. no treatment currently is indicated
    C. monitor CD4 every 3 to 6 months
    D. patient education
    E. all of the above

15. An important role of the AIDS counselor is as

    A. teacher
    B. advisor
    C. support person
    D. interviewer
    E. all of the above

16. All of the following are important objectives of HIV test counseling EXCEPT

    A. facilitating client decision-making skills
    B. providing client education about drugs
    C. encouraging responsible client sexual behavior
    D. encouraging and assisting client in making personal changes in their behavior to reduce their risk of re-exposure
    E. assisting the client in developing and modifying risk reduction plans to maintain behavior change

17. The AIDS counselor must help the client deal with all of the following emotional issues EXCEPT

    A. disclosing HIV status to partner
    B. coping with a positive test result
    C. making decisions about having children
    D. making sexual behavior change
    E. encouraging behavior regarding frequent drug use

18. During short-term counseling sessions, communication skills are the most important tools.
    These skills include

    A. culturally sensitive communication
    B. verbal communication skills
    C. reflective listening
    D. all of the above
    E. none of the above

19. The statement regarding verbal counseling skills that is NOT helpful is:

    A. Elicit more information in less time.
    B. Elicit information in more time so as to gain confidence of the patient.
    C. Express respect and honesty.
    D. Often begin with how, what, where, when, and why.
    E. Ask for information or explanations.

20. HIV confidentiality law requires HIV test counselors to discuss

    A. the nature of AIDS
    B. the nature of HIV-related illness
    C. legal protection against AIDS discrimination
    D. behavior known to pose risk for transmission and contraction of HIV infection
    E. all of the above

21. All of the following are non-HIV-related medical complications of substance abuse EXCEPT

    A. lymphoma of brain
    B. hepatitis
    C. endocarditis
    D. cellulitis
    E. subcutaneous abscesses

22. All of the following statements about HIV/AIDS in women are true EXCEPT:

    A. AIDS has become the number one cause of death for women 20-44 years of age.
    B. AIDS deaths among women have quadrupled in four years.
    C. Women are the fastest growing population with HIV in the United States.
    D. AIDS is one of the five leading causes of death for women.
    E. In New York, AIDS is more common among whites than blacks.

23. The risk factor for female-to-female transmission include

    A. current or former male partner at risk
    B. current or former female partner at risk
    C. history of sharing needles
    D. recipient of artificial insemination
    E. all of the above

24. Clinical manifestations of HIV disease in women include all of the following EXCEPT

    A. chronic vaginal candidiasis
    B. single episode of pharyngitis
    C. cervical dysplasia
    D. frequent outbreak of severe genital herpes
    E. frequent episode of severe PID

25. Recommendations for HIV serologic testing include

    A. persons who have sexually transmitted disease
    B. IV drug users
    C. gay and bisexual men
    D. patients with active tuberculosis
    E. all of the above

KEY (CORRECT ANSWERS)

1. B
2. B
3. E
4. A
5. C

6. A
7. D
8. B
9. E
10. A

11. C
12. E
13. E
14. E
15. E

16. B
17. E
18. D
19. B
20. E

21. A
22. E
23. E
24. B
25. E

TEST 2

DIRECTIONS: Each question or incomplete statement is followed by several suggested answers or completions. Select the one that BEST answers the question or completes the statement. *PRINT THE LETTER OF THE CORRECT ANSWER IN THE SPACE AT THE RIGHT.*

1. The HIGHEST seroprevalence rates of HIV in the United States is among

   A. prostitutes
   B. gay men
   C. hemophiliacs who received clotting factor before 1985
   D. IV drug abusers
   E. partners of HIV-infected persons

2. Among the following, the TRUE statement regarding a patient with HIV positive test is:

   A. 80% of patients will die in the first five years.
   B. 30-50% of patients will go on to develop AIDS in 6 years.
   C. A person with positive test without development of AIDS is not considered infectious.
   D. A person with positive test without development of AIDS is not capable of transmitting the infection to others.
   E. None of the above

3. A 24-year-old male has accidental parental exposure (needle stick) to HIV-infected blood.
   The BEST estimate of the risk of HIV infection following such a single parental exposure is one per _____ exposures.

   A. 10   B. 50   C. 100   D. 250   E. 1,000

4. A drug of choice for prophylaxis of a patient exposed to HIV-contaminated needle is

   A. zidoudine
   B. stavudine
   C. acyclovir
   D. dideoxycytidine
   E. didanosine

5. The prophylaxis should be initiated _____ after exposure.

   A. within one hour and no later than 72 hours
   B. within one week
   C. within one month
   D. within three months
   E. prophylaxis is not required

6. All of the following are true statements regarding prevention of occupational HIV transmission and body substance precautions EXCEPT:

   A. Needles should never be re-capped using both hands.
   B. Gloves should be worn whenever touching mucous membranes or broken skin.
   C. Protective goggles and mask should be avoided if splash exposure is likely.
   D. Gowns should be worn when patient care is expected to soil clothing.
   E. Sharp objects should be deposited into a puncture-proof disposal container as soon as possible.

7. Initial laboratory evaluations of patients with HIV include all of the following EXCEPT

   A. CBC with differential and platelets
   B. base line electrolyte, bun, creatinine, and liver function test
   C. CD4 count, lactate dehydrogenase, and G6-PD
   D. blood culture, urine culture, and CSF culture
   E. VDRL, hepatitis B serologies, and PPD tuberculin test

8. _____ percent of patients with AIDS acquire mai cm-ovium-intracollulare infection in their lifetime.

   A. 100   B. 25-50
   C. 0-5   D. 5-10
   E. 75-90

9. The individuals and institutions authorized to receive HIV-related information under the New York State public health law include all of the following EXCEPT:

   A. An authorized foster care or adoption agency
   B. The patient or a person authorized by law who consented to the test on behalf of the patient
   C. A family friend visiting the patient asks you about the diagnosis
   D. Anyone whom the patient has specifically authorized to receive such information by signing a written release
   E. A committee or organization responsible for reviewing or monitoring a health facility

10. When you assist a client in coping with an HIV test result, you should be prepared to deal with the client's emotions including

    A. disbelief   B. depression
    C. anger   D. fear of death
    E. all of the above

11. A client with positive HIV test results should be told that

    A. the HIV test shows that antibody to HIV is present
    B. a positive test does not mean he has AIDS or will necessarily develop AIDS
    C. he can infect others with HIV
    D. all of the above
    E. none of the above

12. If the client requests a repeat HIV test to confirm his HIV positive status, you will tell him

    A. HIV test is over 98% accurate for detecting HIV antibody
    B. retesting is not considered necessary but will be provided upon his request
    C. that you expect the HIV retest will be positive
    D. none of the above
    E. all of the above

13. If you are counseling a woman with HIV positive status who recently gave birth to a child, you would tell her all of the following EXCEPT:

    A. Her positive status does not necessarily mean that her baby is infected with HIV.
    B. Only 20 to 30% of babies born to HIV positive mothers get the disease.
    C. The baby will test HIV positive for its whole life.
    D. Her baby will test HIV positive at birth if she has antibodies to HIV.
    E. If the baby is not infected, the baby should test negative by 18 to 24 months of age.

14. Children of biological parents who are HIV positive should be told by the counselor that

    A. they should be tested for HIV
    B. infants may become infected with HIV due to maternal/ child transmission
    C. children born with possible maternal/child transmission should be tested immediately after birth
    D. female partners of HIV positive men should be referred for testing and counseling
    E. all of the above

15. An infant is born to a mother who has antibodies to HIV, and tests positive. At what age should you recommend retesting for HIV?

    A. 2 to 4 months
    B. 6 to 8 months
    C. 10 to 12 months
    D. 18 to 24 months
    E. No retesting required

16. Medical management of HIV positive clients includes

    A. regular medical monitoring
    B. testing of immune system
    C. early treatment in view of weak immune system
    D. all of the above
    E. none of the above

17. A comprehensive medical evaluation of a client suffering from HIV include all of the following EXCEPT

    A. test for immune system
    B. complete medical and personal history
    C. detailed physical exam
    D. testing for sexually transmitted diseases
    E. serial lumbar punctures

18. The immune system of HIV positive clients can be strengthened by all of the following EXCEPT

    A. avoiding alcohol and drug abuse
    B. avoiding stress
    C. blood testing weekly
    D. getting regular exercise
    E. eating a balanced diet

19. In advising clients, it would be IMPROPER to   19._____

    A. include the partner or spouse
    B. exclude family members from the counseling
    C. create support groups
    D. give alcohol or drug treatment
    E. give family planning counseling

20. Partner notification should be effected by all of the following methods EXCEPT: 20._____

    A. Such notification should be done through the patient
    B. Through former sex and needle-sharing partner
    C. In case of inability of the client to disclose, client should be coached
    D. People concerned should be made aware of all programs run by the state
    E. A client should be given a written referral for programs in the area

---

KEY (CORRECT ANSWERS)

1.	C	11.	D
2.	B	12.	E
3.	D	13.	C
4.	A	14.	E
5.	A	15.	D
6.	C	16.	D
7.	D	17.	E
8.	B	18.	C
9.	C	19.	B
10.	E	20.	A

MICROBIOLOGY / PATHOLOGY
EXAMINATION SECTION
TEST 1

DIRECTIONS: Each question or incomplete statement is followed by several suggested answers or completions. Select the one that BEST answers the question or completes the statement. *PRINT THE LETTER OF THE CORRECT ANSWER IN THE SPACE AT THE RIGHT.*

1. The tensile strength of a healing wound depends upon   1.____

    A. wound hormones
    B. adequate fluid intake
    C. activation of fibrinolysis
    D. formation of collagen fibers
    E. erythropoietin stimulation of bone marrow

2. The organism which causes Rocky Mountain spotted fever is perpetuated in nature *mainly* in   2.____

    A. lice   B. mites
    C. ticks   D. humans
    E. rabbits

3. Reed-Sternberg cells are pathognomonic of   3.____

    A. typhoid fever
    B. Hodgkin's disease
    C. Burkitt's lymphoma
    D. anterior poliomyelitis
    E. von Recklinghausen's disease

4. Two important "post-streptococcal" diseases are   4.____

    A. impetigo and osteolyelitis
    B. puerperal fever and anthrax
    C. scarlet fever and erysipelas
    D. pharyngitis and the common cold
    E. rheumatic fever and glomerulonephritis

5. Margination of leukocytes refers to   5.____

    A. crowding of the cells into an axial stream
    B. lining up of the cells along the wall of a dilated vessel
    C. an increase in the number of cells at the margin of a wound
    D. abnormal motility of the cells
    E. none of the above

6. A darkfield microscope would be useful in examining blood for   6.____

    A. treponema   B. actinomyces
    C. streptococcus   D. mycobacterium
    E. bacillus anthracis spores

7. The indiscriminate use of broad-spectrum antibiotics is CONTRAINDICATED because they frequently

    A. are extremely nephrotoxic
    B. cause psychogenic symptoms
    C. produce dependency reactions
    D. induce anaphylactoid reactions
    E. interfere with indigenous biota

8. Although the exact mechanism of the formation of calculus is not understood, it is known that the organic matrix of calculus in humans includes

    A. an abundance of microorganisms
    B. *only* an occasional microorganism
    C. *only* the by-products of bacterial metabolism
    D. a fusospirochetal complex
    E. no living microorganisms

9. Hemorrhage may occur in patients with severe liver disease because of a deficiency in

    A. prothrombin
    B. thromboplastin
    C. gamma globulin
    D. calcium ions in the serum
    E. none of the above

10. Measles is transmitted from one person to another via

    A. feces
    B. fomites
    C. insect bites
    D. contaminated water supply
    E. respiratory droplets

11. Hematemesis refers to

    A. nasal hemorrhage
    B. vomiting of blood
    C. blood in the stool
    D. blood in the urine
    E. coughing up blood from the lungs

12. When a rejected allograft is followed by a second allograft from the same donor, the

    A. graft takes
    B. second rejection occurs more rapidly than the first
    C. second rejection occurs more slowly than the first
    D. second rejection occurs in 50 percent of the cases
    E. none of the above

13. In the replication of viral particles, the host cell provides

    A. genetic information, and the virus provides synthetic enzymes
    B. nutrients, and the virus provides metabolic enzymes
    C. metabolic enzymes, and the virus provides genetic information
    D. genetic information, and the virus incorporates nutrients
    E. none of the above

14. The substrate on which streptococcus mutans acts to produce dextrans and levans is

    A. glucose
    B. sucrose
    C. fructose
    D. glycogen
    E. amylopectin

15. Mutations are due to changes in

    A. amino acid sequence of deoxyribonuclease
    B. amino acid sequence of ribonuclease
    C. RNA nucleotide sequence
    D. DNA nucleotide sequence
    E. cell wall peptidoglycan

16. Epithelial pearls and intercellular bridges observed in an infiltrating malignancy are diagnostic of

    A. adenocarcinoma
    B. anaplastic carcinoma
    C. squamous cell carcinoma
    D. undifferentiated carcinoma
    E. transitional cell carcinoma

17. Reducing the number of infectious agents on headrests and operating light handles to an acceptable level is called

    A. asepsis
    B. attenuation
    C. disinfection
    D. sterilization
    E. none of the above

18. An antibacterial substance found in saliva, tears and egg white is

    A. albumin
    B. isozyme
    C. amylase
    D. lysozyme
    E. betalysin

19. A virus which causes two distinct diseases in different age groups is

    A. influenza
    B. measles
    C. smallpox
    D. varicella
    E. Newcastle disease

20. Staphylococci *typically* occur in

    A. pairs
    B. chains
    C. tetrads
    D. irregular clusters
    E. palisade arrangement

21. A protoplast is BEST characterized as a bacterial cell

    A. with a cell wall but free of a capsule
    B. containing a cell wall and a capsule
    C. free of a cell wall and a capsule
    D. uniquely sensitive to penicillin
    E. none of the above

22. A 65-year-old male who demonstrates urinary retention or difficulty in voiding his bladder *most likely* has

    A. malignant neoplasm of the ureter
    B. carcinoma of the prostate
    C. benign prostatic hyperplasia
    D. bladder metastasis of bronchogenic carcinoma
    E. none of the above

23. Of the following, the MOST radiosensitive cell is the

    A. lymphocyte   B. nerve cell
    C. muscle cell   D. cartilage cell
    E. endothelial cell

24. On the basis of histogenesis and transitions observed in clinical cases, there appears to be a relationship between lymphocytic lymphoma and

    A. lymphadenitis
    B. lymphoepithelioma
    C. lymphocytic leukemia
    D. infectious lymphocytosis
    E. infectious mononucleosis

25. Dystrophic calcification of tissue or cells is

    A. secondary to pituitary hypoplasia
    B. associated with high blood calcium
    C. associated with high blood phosphorus
    D. secondary to disease of the tissue affected
    E. none of the above

KEY (CORRECT ANSWERS)

1. D
2. C
3. B
4. E
5. B

6. A
7. E
8. A
9. A
10. E

11. B
12. B
13. C
14. B
15. D

16. C
17. C
18. D
19. D
20. D

21. C
22. C
23. A
24. C
25. D

TEST 2

DIRECTIONS: Each question or incomplete statement is followed by several suggested answers or completions. Select the one that BEST answers the question or completes the statement. *PRINT THE LETTER OF THE CORRECT ANSWER IN THE SPACE AT THE RIGHT.*

1. A positive skin test in an individual who has had tuberculosis is an example of   1.____

   A. atopy
   B. autoimmunity
   C. hypersensitivity
   D. passive immunity
   E. none of the above

2. Rough pneumococci grown in the presence of DNA from smooth pneumococci develop capsules. This is known as   2.____

   A. mutation
   B. conjugation
   C. translation
   D. transduction
   E. transformation

3. The *most likely* mechanism for the increased occurrence of drug-resistant microorganisms is   3.____

   A. R factor transfer of resistance
   B. increased mutation rate
   C. diet of the host
   D. lysogeny
   E. none of the above

4. A disease of childhood characterized by mental retardation, delayed growth and delayed tooth eruption is associated with a deficiency of   4.____

   A. oxytocin
   B. growth hormone
   C. thyroid hormone
   D. testicular hormone
   E. mineralocorticoids

5. A person's blood is mixed separately with A antiserum, B antiserum and Rh positive antiserum. No clumping or agglutination of the red cells occurs. This person has type _____ blood and is Rh _____.   5.____

   A. O, positive
   B. O, negative
   C. AB, positive
   D. AB, negative
   E. A, positive

6. The mechanism of action of quaternary ammonium compounds is against the   6.____

   A. metachromatic granules
   B. cytoplasmic membrane
   C. cell wall
   D. flagella
   E. DNA

7. In general, rickettsia and viruses have in common   7.____

   A. size
   B. filterability
   C. growth environment
   D. method of reproduction
   E. resistance to antibiotics

8. Selective cytotoxicity denotes a drug action which

   A. is easily tested in vitro
   B. affects parasites more strongly than host cells
   C. substitutes a poisonous analogue for an essential nutrient
   D. is limited to bacteria and does not include protozoa
   E. destroys the cell with no effect on the nucleus

9. For uniform staining reaction, morphology and biochemical activity, it is advisable to study bacterial cultures during the _____ phase.

   A. lag
   B. death
   C. stationary
   D. logarithmic
   E. none of the above

10. Endotoxins differ from exotoxins in that endotoxins

    A. are proteins
    B. are heat labile
    C. are highly antigenic
    D. activate complement by the alternate pathway
    E. can be converted into toxoids by treatment with formalin

11. Transformation of mucous-secreting bronchial epithelium to squamous epithelium is an example of

    A. aplasia
    B. anaplasia
    C. dysplasia
    D. metaplasia
    E. hyperplasia

12. The term "nephrosis" *generally* implies renal disease which *primarily* involves the

    A. tubules
    B. glomeruli
    C. renal papillae
    D. renal artery
    E. interstitial connective tissue

13. The mechanism by which most fungi cause disease is

    A. endotoxin production
    B. exotoxin production
    C. lecithinase production
    D. coagulase production
    E. hypersensitivity

14. Hypochromic microcytic anemia is characteristic of

    A. sprue
    B. aplastic anemia
    C. pernicious anemia
    D. iron-deficiency anemia
    E. none of the above

15. The pulmonary neoplasm to which the endocrine effect of hyperparathyroidism is attributed is

    A. squamous cell carcinoma
    B. medullary carcinoma
    C. oat cell carcinoma
    D. pheochromocytoma
    E. adenocarcinoma

16. The medium of choice for growing MOST fungi is   16.____

    A. blood agar
    B. tissue culture
    C. Sabouraud's agar
    D. thioglycollate medium
    E. nutrient agar containing lactophenol cotton blue

17. The chemotactic accumulation of mononuclear cells which occurs at the sites where   17.____
    immune complexes are deposited is *most probably* the result of

    A. C3   B. IgA
    C. IgD   D. IgE
    E. sensitized lymphocytes

18. Bronchopneumonia is characterized by   18.____

    A. inflammation of a bronchus only
    B. organization of alveolar exudate
    C. patchy distribution of lobular inflammation
    D. uniform involvement of the lobe associated with the inflamed bronchus
    E. none of the above

19. Massive necrotizing lesions of the palate in a patient with poorly-controlled diabetes mel-   19.____
    litus are *frequently* related to

    A. mucormycosis   B. blastomycosis
    C. coccidoidomycosis   D. histoplasmosis
    E. cryptococcosis

20. A lysogenic bacterium is one that   20.____

    A. lyses red cells
    B. produces properdin
    C. harbors a temperate bacteriophage
    D. produces lecithinase when incubated anaerobically
    E. produces spheroplasts when incubated anaerobically

21. The effectiveness of autoclaving is BEST determined by   21.____

    A. indicators that change color at elevated temperatures
    B. thermocouples (temperature recording devices)
    C. culturing the water reservoir
    D. culturing bacterial spores
    E. none of the above

22. A patient with shingles (herpes zoster) is *most likely* to have had a previous episode of   22.____

    A. smallpox
    B. chickenpox
    C. autoimmune disease
    D. respiratory syncytial virus infection
    E. trauma to the spinal cord or the nerve roots

23. Herpes simplex virus type 1 is *usually* associated with   23.____

    A. neural lesions   B. genital lesions
    C. cervical carcinoma   D. oral and ocular lesions
    E. none of the above

24. The essential antigen in diplococcus pneumoniae which determines both its virulence   24.____
and its specific type is the

    A. somatic carbohydrate   B. flagellar carbohydrate
    C. thermolabile leukocidin   D. capsular polysaccharide
    E. nucleoprotein structure

25. In Bruton's agammaglobulinemia, adequate host defense mechanisms exist for resistance to   25.____

    A. virus infections   B. fungal infections
    C. bacterial infections   D. nonpathogenic bacteria
    E. none of the above

KEY (CORRECT ANSWERS)

1.	C	11.	D
2.	E	12.	A
3.	A	13.	E
4.	C	14.	D
5.	B	15.	C
6.	B	16.	C
7.	C	17.	A
8.	B	18.	C
9.	D	19.	A
10.	D	20.	C

21.	D
22.	B
23.	D
24.	D
25.	A

MICROBIOLOGY / PATHOLOGY
EXAMINATION SECTION
TEST 1

DIRECTIONS: Each question or incomplete statement is followed by several suggested answers or completions. Select the one that BEST answers the question or completes the statement. *PRINT THE LETTER OF THE CORRECT ANSWER IN THE SPACE AT THE RIGHT.*

1. The early bronchial mucosal alteration *most likely* to be observed in cigarette smokers is   1.____

    A. dysplasia
    B. neoplasia
    C. metaplasia
    D. hypoplasia
    E. hyperplasia

2. A 65-year-old male who demonstrates urinary retention or difficulty in voiding his bladder *most likely* has   2.____

    A. carcinoma of the prostate
    B. benign prostatic hyperplasia
    C. malignant neoplasm of the ureter
    D. bladder metastasis of bronchogenic carcinoma
    E. polyps

3. Interstitial pulmonary inflammation is MOST characteristic of   3.____

    A. lobar pneumonia
    B. viral pneumonia
    C. bronchial asthma
    D. bronchopneumonia
    E. pleurisy

4. Aerobic organotrophic (or heterotrophic) bacteria which oxidize a substrate to CO_2 and H_2O use, in the final electron transport, enzymes containing   4.____

    A. cytochromes
    B. coenzyme A
    C. ribose nucleic acid
    D. pyridine nucleotides
    E. flavin adenine dinucleotide

5. The etiology of acute diffuse glomerulonephritis seems to be   5.____

    A. circulatory deficiency associated with prolonged shock
    B. bacteremia with localization of organisms in kidney tissue
    C. injury of glomeruli by exogenous inorganic toxins
    D. degenerative changes induced by sclerotic alterations of blood vessels
    E. allergic reaction of glomerular and vascular tissue to beta-hemolytic streptococcal products

6. Following the initial transient vasoconstriction, the NEXT vascular reaction to injury in the sequence of events in inflammation is   6.____

    A. margination of leukocytes
    B. dilation of blood vessels
    C. increased capillary permeability
    D. movement of leukocytes toward the irritant
    E. phagocytosis of bacteria and other particles

7. Recurrent aphthae resemble recurrent herpes in that

   A. symptoms are similar
   B. life-long immunity results
   C. vesicles occur with both diseases
   D. intranuclear inclusion bodies are present
   E. circulating antibodies to the etiologic agents may be demonstrated

8. The BEST evidence for a causal relationship between a nasal carrier of staphylococci and a staphylococcal infection in a hospital patient is the demonstration that the organisms from both individuals

   A. are coagulase-positive
   B. are penicillin resistant
   C. are of the same phage type
   D. are aureus-type staphylococci
   E. produce hemolysis, liquefy gelation and ferment mannitol

9. For the MAJORITY of individuals, the INITIAL infection with herpes simplex virus results in

   A. encephalitis as a young adult
   B. a dermal rash in childhood
   C. herpes labialis in puberty
   D. a subclinical disease
   E. genital herpes

10. The radiosensitivity of tissue is MOST closely related to the

    A. mitotic rate
    B. nuclear cytoplasmic ratio
    C. RNA content of the cytoplasm
    D. size of the cells that make up the tissue
    E. ionization density of the primary irradiation

11. The MOST conspicuous clinical sign of right-sided heart failure is

    A. hypertension
    B. mitral stenosis
    C. pulmonary edema
    D. systemic venous congestion
    E. brown induration of the lung

12. An example of hypoplasia is the

    A. absence of an organ
    B. underdevelopment of an organ
    C. acquired reduction in size of an organ
    D. increase in number of cells of an organ
    E. none of the above

13. The renal disease *most commonly* related to hypertension is   13._____

    A. renal atresia
    B. nephrosclerosis
    C. acute pyelonephritis
    D. chronic pyelonephritis
    E. none of the above

14. Myxedema is an endocrine disturbance resulting from   14._____

    A. secondary hyperparathyroidism in children
    B. primary hyperparathyroidism in adults
    C. hyperpituitarism in adults
    D. hypothyroidism in children
    E. hypothyroidism in adults

15. Some investigators believe streptococci are predominant in the etiology of caries because streptococci   15._____

    A. produce caries in germ-free rats when introduced as monocontaminants
    B. are predominant in saliva
    C. are beta-hemolytic
    D. contain M protein
    E. all of the above

16. Detergents kill bacteria by interfering with the function of the cell   16._____

    A. wall
    B. nucleus
    C. capsule
    D. membrane
    E. cytoplasm

17. Massive necrotizing lesions of the palate in a patient with poorly-controlled diabetes mellitus are *frequently* related to   17._____

    A. phycomycosis
    B. blastomycosis
    C. histoplasmosis
    D. cryptococcosis
    E. coccidoidomycosis

18. An example of an endogenous bacterial infection is   18._____

    A. trachoma
    B. Weil's disease
    C. leptospirosis
    D. salmonellosis
    E. actinomycosis

19. MOST forms of lung cancer arise from the   19._____

    A. peribronchial lymph nodes
    B. lining epithelium of the alveoli
    C. lining epithelium of the tracheobronchial tree
    D. submucosal glands of the tracheobronchial tree
    E. pleural sacs

20. Rheumatic fever, scleroderma and rheumatoid arthritis exhibit _____ degeneration.   20._____

    A. fatty
    B. amyloid
    C. hyaline
    D. fibrinoid
    E. epithelial

21. A bacterium well known for its large polysaccharide capsule is   21.____

    A. clostridium tetani
    B. staphylococcus aureus
    C. hemophilus influenzae
    D. streptococcus pneumoniae
    E. mycobacterium tuberculosis

22. Recurrent herpes labialis occurs in those people who   22.____

    A. have had no previous contact with herpesvirus
    B. have been infected with herpesvirus but who fail to produce antibodies against the virus
    C. have been infected with herpesvirus and who have antibodies against the virus
    D. are hypersensitive to herpesvirus
    E. have little resistance

23. Cellular swelling is one of the MOST common changes observed in tissues obtained at autopsy. Its occurrence   23.____

    A. proves only that the circulation was deficient
    B. is useful only in identifying certain infections
    C. usually indicates the action of specific etiologic agents
    D. assists in evaluating the nutritional status of the organ involved
    E. is of little practical diagnostic importance

24. IgG antibodies have a half-life of *approximately*   24.____

    A. 20 minutes   B. 1 hour
    C. 1 day   D. 1 week
    E. 1 month

25. The MOST reliable finding in the serodiagnosis of an acute infectious disease is   25.____

    A. high antibody titer
    B. rising antibody titer
    C. falling antibody titer
    D. positive complement-fixation test
    E. positive tuberculin-type skin test

KEY (CORRECT ANSWERS)

1. C
2. B
3. B
4. A
5. E

6. B
7. A
8. C
9. D
10. A

11. D
12. B
13. B
14. E
15. A

16. D
17. A
18. E
19. C
20. D

21. D
22. C
23. E
24. E
25. B

TEST 2

DIRECTIONS: Each question or incomplete statement is followed by several suggested answers or completions. Select the one that BEST answers the question or completes the Statement. *PRINT THE LETTER OF THE CORRECT ANSWER IN THE SPACE AT THE RIGHT.*

1. The end-product of glucose metabolism by streptococcus mutans is

   A. lactate
   B. pyruvate
   C. citric acid
   D. a combination of carbon dioxide and water
   E. none of the above

   1.____

2. Myocardial infarction results in

   A. coagulation necrosis
   B. liquefaction necrosis
   C. amyloid degeneration
   D. Zenker's degeneration
   E. mucinous degeneration

   2.____

3. The cellular infiltrate in a fully-developed delayed hypersensitivity reaction consists *mainly* of

   A. mast cells and erythrocytes
   B. macrophages and lymphocytes
   C. macrophages and polymorphonuclear leukocytes
   D. plasma cells and polymorphonuclear leukocytes
   E. none of the above

   3.____

4. Active passage of leukocytes through capillary walls is accomplished by means of

   A. desmosome lysis
   B. endothelial pores
   C. pinocytotic vesicles
   D. loosened interendothelial junctions
   E. none of the above

   4.____

5. The chemotactic accumulation at the site of immune complex deposition is a result of

   A. steroids
   B. histamine
   C. complement
   D. antihistamines
   E. analgesics

   5.____

6. The *primary* value of soap lies in its

   A. sporocidal action
   B. bactericidal action
   C. bacteriostatic action
   D. removal of microbes from skin surfaces
   E. detergent properties

   6.____

7. The epithelial change MOST predictive of cancer is

   A. acanthosis
   B. dysplasia
   C. metaplasia
   D. parakeratosis
   E. hyperkeratosis

8. The MOST reliable postmortem indicator of left ventricular cardiac failure is

   A. ascites
   B. venous congestion
   C. enlargement of the spleen
   D. peripheral edema of the ankles
   E. chronic passive congestion of the lungs

9. Histoplasmosis is a highly infectious mycotic disease that is characterized microscopically by

   A. intranuclear inclusion bodies
   B. flask-shaped ulcers of the ileum
   C. intracytoplasmic microorganisms in the R-E system
   D. focal abscesses of the liver and the intestinal tract
   E. none of the above

10. "Late" proteins synthesized in viral replication include

    A. DNA polymerases
    B. virus structural proteins
    C. proteins that inhibit host cell protein synthesis
    D. proteins that cause cessation of host cell RNA synthesis
    E. none of the above

11. A thymectomized animal or a person with an inborn deficiency of thymus *usually* has

    A. no lymph nodes
    B. no phagocytic cells
    C. a selective deficiency of IgE
    D. total absence of circulating antibodies
    E. decreased or absent delayed-type hypersensitivity

12. In transduction, DNA is transferred from donor cell to recipient cell by

    A. a plasmid
    B. an episome
    C. a bacteriophage
    D. purified nucleic acid
    E. none of the above

13. The MOST common cause of hepatomegaly without other distinctive signs and symptoms is

    A. ascites
    B. hematoma
    C. hepatitis
    D. neoplasia
    E. fatty change

14. Arguments against indiscriminate use of antibiotics as chemotherapeutic agents include
     I. toxic effects of the antibiotics
     II. allergic reactions induced in patients
     III. development of drug resistance by an infectious agent
     IV. secondary effects experienced due to creation of an imbalance in the normal body flora
     V. alteration of the immune response
    The CORRECT answer is:

    A. I, II, III
    B. I, II, IV, V
    C. II, IV, V
    D. III, IV, V
    E. I, II, III, IV, V

15. Irreversible pathologic changes include
     I. fatty degeneration
     II. hydropic degeneration
     III. autolysis
     IV. coagulative necrosis
    The CORRECT answer is:

    A. I, III
    B. I, III, IV
    C. II, III
    D. II, IV
    E. III, IV

16. Seeding or transplantation metastasis would be *likely* in carcinomas of the
     I. tongue
     II. stomach
     III. ovary
     IV. skin
     V. large bowel
    The CORRECT answer is:

    A. I, II, III
    B. I, IV, V
    C. II, III, IV
    D. II, III, V
    E. II, IV, V

17. Which of the following therapeutic agents are classed as broad-spectrum antibiotics?
     I. Tetracycline
     II. Chloromycetin
     III. Dihydrostreptomycin
     IV. Penicillin
     V. Isoniazid
    The CORRECT answer is:

    A. I, II
    B. I, II, IV, V
    C. I, III, V
    D. I, V
    E. II, III, IV

18. Oversecretion of which of the following hormones causes phosphate diuresis and results in elevated serum calcium?

    A. Thyroxin
    B. Cortisone
    C. Pituitrin
    D. Parathormone
    E. Guanine

19. Of the following bone diseases, which is of endocrine etiology?

    A. Myeloma
    B. Acromegaly
    C. Osteopetrosis
    D. Paget's disease
    E. Monostotic fibrous dysplasia

20. A Ghon focus (tubercle) is a

    A. primary lung lesion in the periphery
    B. lesion occurring only in the bronchi
    C. fibrous lesion in 50 percent of the bronchi
    D. secondary lung lesion in over 90 percent of adults
    E. none of the above

21. Which of the following antibiotics is effective in treating candidiasis?

    A. Nystatin   B. Bacitracin
    C. Penicillin   D. Tetracycline
    E. Griseofulvin

22. The presence of which of the following factors in viruses makes protective vaccines a possibility?

    A. Lipids   B. Enzymes
    C. Protein coat   D. Polysaccharide
    E. Methylcytosine

23. Which of the following statements is CORRECT regarding a patient recovered from hepatitis type B infection?

    A. The virus will be excreted in the feces.
    B. The patient is a good candidate for blood donation.
    C. The patient will have protective immunity to all viral hepatitides.
    D. Detection of hepatitis B antigen in serum is indicative of the carrier state.
    E. None of the above

24. Infectious mononucleosis is caused by the _____ virus.

    A. verruca   B. rubella
    C. rubeola   D. Epstein-Barr
    E. varicella-zoster

25. Which of the following viruses is suspect in cervical cancer?

    A. HVH-1   B. HVH-2
    C. EBV   D. C-type particles
    E. ADP

KEY (CORRECT ANSWERS)

1.	A	11.	E
2.	A	12.	C
3.	B	13.	E
4.	B	14.	E
5.	C	15.	E
6.	D	16.	D
7.	B	17.	A
8.	E	18.	D
9.	C	19.	B
10.	B	20.	A

21. A
22. C
23. D
24. D
25. B

EXAMINATION SECTION
TEST 1

DIRECTIONS: Each question or incomplete statement is followed by several suggested answers or completions. Select the one that BEST answers the question or completes the statement. *PRINT THE LETTER OF THE CORRECT ANSWER IN THE SPACE AT THE RIGHT.*

1. The difference between the boiling point and the freezing point of water on the Fahrenheit scale is

    A. 0°   B. 100°   C. 112°   D. 180°

2. All amino acids contain

    A. calcium and carbon
    B. hydrogen and nitrogen
    C. iron and oxygen
    D. manganese and phosphorus

3. Acids and bases combine to form compounds known as

    A. colloids   B. salts   C. solids   D. solutions

4. $C_6H_{12}O_6$ represents the formula for a(n)

    A. protein   B. salt   C. sugar   D. oil

5. The soil pH which is suitable for MOST garden crops varies between

    A. 2 and 5   B. 5 and 8   C. 8 and 11   D. 11 and 14

6. The farmer who plants peas, clover or alfalfa improves the soil PRIMARILY by increasing the available amount of

    A. carbon   B. hydrogen   C. nitrogen   D. oxygen

7. Phenolphthalein is *generally* used as a(n)

    A. buffer
    B. drying agent
    C. emulsifying agent
    D. indicator

8. Of the following, the one classified as a compound is

    A. aluminum   B. ammonia   C. nitrogen   D. sulfur

9. The process in which a liquid is vaporized and then condensed is called

    A. crystallization
    B. decantation
    C. distillation
    D. filtration

10. The formula *4-8-4* used in fertilizers refers to

    A. calcium, magnesium, and sulfur
    B. calcium, nitrogen, and phosphorus
    C. nitrogen, phosphorus, and potassium
    D. nitrogen, potassium, and sodium

11. The CHIEF source of fuel energy for the living cell are

    A. carbohydrates and fats
    B. carbohydrates and proteins
    C. fats and proteins
    D. water and carbohydrates

12. The structures of the human alimentary canal, in the order in which food passes through them, are as follows: first the mouth and throat, and then, IN ORDER, the

    A. esophagus, the small intestine, the large intestine, and the stomach
    B. esophagus, the stomach, the large intestine, and the small intestine
    C. esophagus, the stomach, the small intestine, and the large intestine
    D. stomach, the large intestine, the small intestine, and the esophagus

13. Pepsin is a stomach enzyme which

    A. changes fats to fatty acids
    B. converts starches to sugars
    C. curdles milk
    D. reduces proteins to peptides

14. The substance responsible for the clotting of human blood is known as

    A. fibrinogen   B. hemoglobin
    C. plasma   D. serum

15. Of the following statements regarding endocrine glands, the one which is NOT true is that

    A. endocrine glands have tubes or ducts to discharge their products to areas of use
    B. hormones are produced in endocrine glands
    C. the adrenal gland is an example of an endocrine gland
    D. the secretions of endocrine glands may be found in the bloodstream

16. The enzyme responsible for breaking fat and fat-like substances into glycerol and fatty acids is

    A. amylase   B. coagulase   C. lipase   D. oxidase

17. An acute x-ray dose of 600 roentgens applied to the entire body is

    A. insignificant except in the case of persons with an abnormally low level of tolerance to x-rays
    B. nearly always fatal
    C. severe in the view of some radiologists and should be avoided as a regular matter unless a person is employed as an x-ray technician
    D. tolerable in the average person, but such doses should not be applied more than once monthly

18. Radiations may cause cancer, yet radiations are used to treat cancer.
    This statement is

    A. *false;* radiations cannot cause cancer
    B. *false;* radiations cannot injure cancerous cells

C. *true;* radiations injure malignant cells but not healthy cells
D. *true;* radiations injure malignant cells without doing proportionate harm to non-malignant cells

19. The uranium-238 atom contains 92 protons and 146 neutrons. The number of electrons in the U-238 atom is

   A. 54   B. 92   C. 146   D. 238

20. The nucleus of the uranium-238 atom contains

   A. electrons and neutrons
   B. electrons and protons
   C. neutrons and protons
   D. neutrons only

21. Assume that a sample of radium with an atomic weight of 226 contains 250,000 atoms. Assume further that the half-life ($T_{1/2}$) of the radium is 1,600 years.
   This means MOST NEARLY that in

   A. 1,600 years 125,000 atoms of the radium sample will have decayed
   B. 1,600 years the portion of the sample which will have decayed can be expressed by the formula $T_{1/2} = 250,000/226$
   C. 3,200 years the portion of the sample which will have decayed can be expressed by the formula $T_{1/2} = 250,000/226$
   D. 3,200 years the radium sample will have decayed completely

22. The scientist who demonstrated that smallpox could be prevented by inoculating the skin of humans with material from cowpox lesions was

   A. Edward Jenner
   B. Robert Koch
   C. Joseph Meister
   D. Theodor Schwann

23. Staphylococci appear under microscopic examinations as

   A. four cells arranged as a square
   B. irregular clusters resembling bunches of grapes
   C. pairs of cells
   D. rows of cells, beadlike or chainlike

24. *Phenol coefficient* refers to a measure of the

   A. amount of phenol which may be added to food for use as a preservative
   B. effectiveness of a disinfectant in relation to phenol
   C. percentage of carbolic acid found in solutions containing phenol
   D. rapidity with which phenol destroys capsulated bacterial cells

25. The Schick test is used to determine susceptibility to

   A. diphtheria
   B. smallpox
   C. tetanus
   D. typhoid fever

26. Infectious hepatitis is a disease caused by

   A. bacteria
   B. protozoa
   C. rickettsiae
   D. viruses

27. *Phagocytes* are
    A. antigens which are used in the production of antibodies
    B. bacteria which destroy red blood cells
    C. cells in the human body which protect it from infection
    D. pathogens which may be present during coughing and sneezing

28. The Breed method is generally used in the bacteriological examination of
    A. meat   B. milk   C. soil   D. water

29. The magnifying power of a microscope may be determined by
    A. adding the power of the objective to the power of the eyepiece
    B. dividing the power of the eyepiece into the power of the objective
    C. multiplying the power of the eyepiece by the power of the objective
    D. subtracting the power of the eyepiece from the power of the objective

30. The statement regarding viruses which is NOT true is that they
    A. are all parasites
    B. are responsible for poliomyelitis
    C. contain desoxyribonucleic acid
    D. grow in animals but not in plants

Questions 31-35.

DIRECTIONS: For each of Questions 31 through 35, select the letter preceding the word whose meaning is MOST NEARLY the same as that of the capitalized word.

31. NOXIOUS
    A. gaseous   B. harmful   C. soothing   D. repulsive

32. PYOGENIC
    A. disease producing   B. fever producing
    C. pus forming   D. water forming

33. RENAL
    A. brain   B. heart   C. kidney   D. stomach

34. ENDEMIC
    A. epidemic
    B. endermic
    C. endoblast
    D. peculiar to a particular people or locality, as a disease

35. MACULATION
    A. reticulation   B. inoculation
    C. maturation   D. defilement

KEY (CORRECT ANSWERS)

1. D
2. B
3. B
4. C
5. B

6. C
7. D
8. B
9. C
10. C

11. A
12. C
13. D
14. A
15. A

16. C
17. B
18. D
19. B
20. C

21. A
22. A
23. B
24. B
25. A

26. D
27. C
28. B
29. C
30. D

31. B
32. C
33. C
34. D
35. D

TEST 2

DIRECTIONS: Each question or incomplete statement is followed by several suggested answers or completions. Select the one that BEST answers the question or completes the statement. *PRINT THE LETTER OF THE CORRECT ANSWER IN THE SPACE AT THE RIGHT.*

1. The immunity found in individuals who have recovered from measles is termed _____ acquired _____ immunity.

    A. artificially; active
    B. artificially; passive
    C. naturally; active
    D. naturally; passive

    1.____

2. Decomposition of fresh or cold storage meats can be detected BEST by

    A. noting absence of surface moisture
    B. noting presence of *off* odors
    C. noting warmth when touched
    D. observing discoloration

    2.____

3. Bacterial control of shellfish and shellfish growing areas is being based increasingly in this country upon the density of the Escherichia coli organisms in the waters from which shellfish are collected.
The BEST reason for this is that

    A. E. coli are virulent pathogens which produce serious diseases in man
    B. the density of E. coli in water is relatively easy to determine by shellfish fishermen
    C. the presence of E. coli is an indicator of the presence of human wastes in the water
    D. shellfish which ingest E. coli have objectionable odors which canning cannot remove

    3.____

4. Proper cleaning of dairy utensils entails rinsing with

    A. cold or lukewarm water followed by scrubbing with a detergent solution
    B. cold or lukewarm water followed by scrubbing with hot soapy water
    C. hot water followed by scrubbing with a detergent solution
    D. hot water followed by scrubbing with hot soapy water

    4.____

5. Of the following, the MOST accurate statement regarding the use of chlorine in the purification of public water supplies is:

    A. A small amount of residual chlorine in the water is desirable
    B. Chlorine will destroy most bacteria in the water with the exception of the coliform organisms
    C. The amount of chlorine added to water should be less than the *chlorine demand* of the water
    D. The use of chlorine in public water supplies should be resorted to only in cases of emergency

    5.____

6. Pasteurization entails the heating of milk to AT LEAST _____ for _____ minutes.

    A. 143° F; 15   B. 143° F; 30   C. 161° F; 15   D. 161° F; 30

    6.____

7. The pH value of water is of considerable significance when chlorinating swimming pools. The reason for this is that chlorine functions BEST as a bactericide when the pH value of the water is

   A. *high;* also, a high pH water value reduces or prevents eye smarting
   B. *high;* however, a high pH water value increases the possibility of eye smarting
   C. *low;* also, a low pH water value reduces or prevents eye smarting
   D. *low;* however, a low pH water value increases the possibility of eye smarting

8. A test commonly used for determining the presence of chlorine in water is the _____ test.

   A. orthotolidine   B. phosphatase
   C. TPI   D. Weil-Felix

9. The chemical which is added to water samples from chlorinated swimming pools to neutralize residual chlorine is sodium

   A. bromide   B. carbonate
   C. hydroxide   D. thiosulfate

10. Some years ago, the city experienced an outbreak of food poisoning from potato salad which was kept in an enameled utensil. The vinegar present in the potato salad dissolved a sufficient quantity of a certain substance found in the enamelware to cause poisoning. The name of the offending substance was

    A. antimony   B. arsenic   C. cyanide   D. zinc

11. The common housefly, Musca Domestica, is a(n)

    A. biting insect which does not transmit disease
    B. biting insect which may transmit disease
    C. insect which does not bite and does not transmit disease
    D. insect which does not bite but may transmit disease

12. The name of the substance which it has been suggested be added to *sleeping medicines* to induce vomiting in the event of an overdose is

    A. chlorpromazine   B. ipecac
    C. reserpine   D. seconal

13. The statement which BEST describes DDT is: DDT is

    A. a contact insect poison
    B. an instantaneous poison
    C. effective against all insects
    D. non-toxic to humans

14. The application of 10% DDT dust to rat runways and burrows is

    A. *advisable,* since it will serve as an effective rodenticide
    B. *advisable,* since it will serve to kill fleas which infest rats
    C. *inadvisable,* since DDT in such amounts stimulates rat growth
    D. *inadvisable,* since rats will be forced to use alternate runways and burrows making their elimination more difficult

15. Oligodynamic action refers to the

   A. ability of extremely small amounts of certain metals to exert a lethal effect upon bacteria
   B. change in levels of chlorine dilution brought about by evaporation
   C. discoloration of tiles in swimming pools due to the excessive mineral content of hard water
   D. removal of organic materials from water by means of sedimentation and filtration

16. The term *BOD*, as used in sewage disposal, refers MOST NEARLY to the

   A. consumption of oxygen by microorganisms engaged in the decomposition of organic material
   B. contamination of oysters and other shellfish by pathogenic bacteria making them unsafe for human consumption
   C. formation of finely suspended sewage material due to vigorous aeration by powerful pumps
   D. removal of suspended or floating objects from raw sewage by screening

Questions 17-22.

DIRECTIONS: Questions 17 through 22 are based on the Health Code.

17. Assume that the applicant for a Health Department permit is under 21 years of age. The statement which BEST applies to such applicant is:

   A. Age is not a factor in the issuance of permits
   B. The applicant may be issued a permit provided he is 18 years of age or over if the commissioner waives the age requirement
   C. The establishment of an age requirement for various permits is left solely to the discretion of the commissioner, who may fix any age requirement he deems appropriate
   D. Under no circumstances may a permit be issued to a person under 21 years of age

18. Assume that a person enters a neighborhood pharmacy and asks that a barbiturate be sold to him. He gives the attending pharmacist the name of his physician and states that he does not have the physician's written prescription for such barbiturate with him.
   In such a case, the pharmacist

   A. may dispense a small amount of the barbiturate without requiring a physician's prescription
   B. may dispense the barbiturate in any amount the pharmacist deems reasonable provided the person is either personally known to the pharmacist or presents proper identification
   C. may telephone the physician and accept the physician's oral prescription subject to the physician's later submission of a written prescription
   D. must insist that he be given the physician's written prescription before he dispenses a barbiturate in any quantity

19. A restaurant owner keeps and houses a cat in his restaurant in order to minimize the danger of rat infestation. He also permits patrons to bring their dogs into his restaurant. The CORRECT statement concerning these actions is that the Health Code _____ the owner to keep his cat on the premises _____ visiting the restaurant with their dogs.

    A. permits; and is silent with respect to patrons
    B. permits; but prohibits patrons from
    C. prohibits; and prohibits patrons from
    D. prohibits; but is silent with respect to patrons

20. The Health Code provides that utensils, such as knives, forks, spoons, cups, and saucers, used in the preparation and service of food are to be cleaned after each use. The Code provides that such cleaning shall consist of _____ cleaning(s) with a suitable detergent in clean hot water followed by _____ rinsing(s).

    A. *one*; *one*
    B. *one*; *two* successive
    C. *two* successive; *one*
    D. *two* successive; *two* successive

21. The owner of a meat market uses certain dyes which impart color to meat. The use of such coloring matter is

    A. absolutely prohibited
    B. permitted if the owner displays a sign which informs consumers that he uses coloring matter
    C. permitted only if the coloring matter is applied to ground beef and to no other meat
    D. prohibited unless such use complies with the provisions of the Federal Meat Inspection Act

22. Homogenized milk is milk which has been subjected to a treatment so that after 48 hours of quiescent storage the percent of butter fat in the upper one-tenth portion of a container will NOT exceed the percentage of butter fat in the remaining portion of the container by more than

    A. 5%   B. 10%   C. 15%   D. 20%

23. The Health Code names certain chemicals which, under stated circumstances, may be added to the drinking water supply within a building for anti-corrosion or anti-scaling purposes.
    Of the following chemicals, the one which is NOT specifically authorized for this purpose is

    A. calcium bicarbonate   B. calcium hydroxide
    C. sodium carbonate   D. sodium hydroxide

24. The Code provides that water in swimming pools must meet a certain standard of clarity. This standard is based on the

    A. addition of a chemical to the water which causes a color change if the water does not meet the prescribed standard
    B. measurement by the laboratory of the turbidity of a sample of pool water

C. use of a black disc, six inches in diameter
D. visual inspection by a sanitarian without the use of any aids or devices

Questions 25-27.

DIRECTIONS: Questions 25 through 27 are to be answered SOLELY on the basis of the following passage.

The first laws prohibiting tampering with foods and selling unwholesome provisions were enacted in ancient times. Early Mosaic and Egyptian laws governed the handling of meat. Greek and Roman laws attempted to prevent the watering of wine. In 200 B.C., India provided for the punishment of adulterators of grains and oils. In the same era, China had agents to prohibit the making of spurious articles and the defrauding of purchasers. Most of our food laws, however, came to us as a heritage from our European forebears.

In early times, foods were few and very simple, and trade existed mostly through barter. Such cheating as did occur was crude and easily detected by the prospective buyer. In the Middle Ages, traders and merchants began to specialize and united themselves into guilds. One of the earliest was called the Pepperers – the spice traders of the day. The Pepperers soon absorbed the grocers and in England got a charter from the king as the Grocer's Company. They set up an ethical code designed to protect the integrity and quality of the spices and other foods sold. Later they appointed a corps of food inspectors to test and certify the merchandise sold to and by the grocers. These men were the first public food inspectors of England.

Pepper is a good example of trade practices that brought about the need for the food inspectors. The demand for pepper was widespread. Its price was high; it was handled by various people during its long journey from the Spice Islands to the grocer's shelf. Each handler had opportunity to debase it; the grinders had the best chance since adulterants could not be detected by methods then available. Worthless barks and seeds, iron ore, charcoal, nutshells, and olive pits were ground along with the berries.

Bread was another food that offered temptation to unscrupulous persons. The most common cheating practice was short weighing but at times the flour used contained ground dried peas or beans.

25. Of the following, the MOST suitable title for the foregoing passage would be: 25.___

   A. Consumer Pressure and Pure Food Laws
   B. Practices Which Brought About the Need for Food Inspectors
   C. Substances Commonly Used as Pepper Adulterants
   D. The Role Played By Pepper as a Spice and as a Preservative

26. The statement BEST supported by the above passage is: 26.___

   A. Food inspectors employed by the Pepperers were responsible for detecting the presence of ground peas in flour
   B. The first guild to be formed in the Middle Ages was known as the Pepperers
   C. The Pepperers were chartered by the king and in accordance with his instructions set up an ethical code
   D. There were persons other than those who handled spices exclusively who became members of the Pepperers

27. The statement BEST supported by the above passage is: 27.___

   A. Early laws of England forbade the addition of adulterants to flour
   B. Egyptian laws of ancient times concerned themselves with meat handling

C. India provided for the punishment of persons adding ground berries and olive pits to spices
D. The Greeks and Romans succeeded in preventing the watering of wine

Questions 28-30.

DIRECTIONS: Questions 28 through 30 are to be answered SOLELY on the basis of the following passage.

Water can purify itself up to a point, by natural processes, but there is a limit to the pollution load that a stream can handle. Self-purification, a complicated process, is brought about by a combination of physical, chemical, and biological factors. The process is the same in all bodies of water, but its intensity is governed by varying environment conditions.

The time required for self-purification is governed by the degree of pollution and the character of the stream. In a large stream, many days of flow may be required for a partial purification. In clean, flowing streams, the water is usually saturated with dissolved purification. In clean, flowing streams, the water is usually saturated with dissolved oxygen, absorbed from the atmosphere and given off by green water plants. The solids of sewage and other wastes are dispersed when they enter the stream and eventually settle. Bacteria in the water and in the wastes themselves begin the process of breaking down the unstable wastes. The process uses up the dissolved oxygen in the water, upon which fish and other aquatic life also depend.

Streams offset the reduction of dissolved oxygen by absorbing it from the air and from oxygen-producing aquatic plants. This replenishment permits the bacteria to continue working on the wastes and the purification process to advance. Replenishment takes place rapidly in a swiftly flowing, turbulent stream because waves provide greater surface areas through which oxygen can be absorbed. Relatively motionless ponds or deep, sluggish streams require more time to renew depleted oxygen.

When large volumes of wastes are discharged into a stream, the water becomes murky. Sunlight no longer penetrates to the water plants, which normally contribute to the oxygen supply through photosynthesis, and the plants die. If the volume of pollution, in relation to the amount of water in the stream and the speed of flow, is so great that the bacteria use the oxygen more rapidly than re-aeration occurs, only putrifying types of bacteria can survive, and the natural process of self-purification is slowed. So the stream becomes foul smelling and looks greasy. Fish and other aquatic life disappear.

28. According to the above passage, if the proportion of wastes to stream water is very high, then the 28.____

   A. amount of dissolved oxygen in the stream increases
   B. death of all bacteria in wastes becomes a certainty
   C. stream will probably look greasy
   D. turbulence of the stream is increased

29. The one of the following which is NOT mentioned in the above passage as a factor in water self-purification is the 29.____

   A. ability of sunlight to penetrate water
   B. percentage of oxygen found in the air
   C. presence of bacteria in waste materials
   D. speed and turbulence of the stream

30. Of the following, the MOST suitable title for the above passage would be: 30.___
    A. Oxygen Requirements of Fish and Other Aquatic Life
    B. Streams as Carriers of Waste Materials
    C. The Function of Bacteria in the Disintegration of Wastes
    D. The Self-purification of Water

Questions 31-32.

DIRECTIONS: Questions 31 and 32 are to be answered SOLELY on the basis of the following passage.

Processing by quick freezing has expanded rapidly. The consumption of frozen fruits and vegetables (on a fresh-equivalent basis) was about 8 pounds per capita annually in the years immediately before the Second World War. It exceeded 200 pounds in 2008.

One example of this growth is frozen concentrated orange juice. From the beginning of commercial production in Florida during the 2005-2006 season, the pack of frozen concentrated orange juice has grown until it amounted to more than 320 million gallons in the 2008-2009 season. That is enough juice, when reconstituted, to supply every person in this country with about 160 average-size servings.

Another striking change in the pattern of food consumption is the sharp increase in consumption of broilers or fryers, young chickens of either sex, usually 8-10 weeks old, and weighing about three pounds.

The commercial production of broilers has increased more than 500 percent since 2006. The number produced exceeded 1.6 billion birds in 2008. On a per capita basis, broiler consumption was about 20 pounds annually (ready-to-cook equivalent basis). This is roughly one-fourth as much as per capita consumption of beef and nearly one-third as large as per capita consumption of pork. Consumption of broilers in the years just after the Second World War was less than one-tenth as large as the consumption of either beef or pork.

Among the factors responsible for this rapid growth are developments in breeding that led to faster gains in weight, lower prices in relation to other meat, and improvements in methods of preparing broilers for market. When broilers, like other poultry, were retailed in an uneviscerated form, dressed broilers could be held for only limited periods. Consequently, birds were shipped to market live, and dressing operations took place mostly in or near terminal markets - the centers of population.

Thus, it is that consumers benefit both from the variety of products available at all seasons of the year and from the many forms in which these products are sold.

31. According to the foregoing passage, the number of broilers produced in 2006 was MOST NEARLY 31.___

    A. 320,000,000   B. 1,200,000,000
    C. 4,000,000,000   D. 5,200,000,000

32. According to the above passage, the per capita annual consumption of frozen fruits and vegetables immediately following the end of World War II 32.___

    A. cannot be determined from the above passage
    B. was 16 percent of the per capita consumption of 2008
    C. was most nearly in excess of 200 pounds
    D. was most nearly 8 pounds

Questions 33-35.

DIRECTIONS: For each of Questions 33 through 35, select the letter preceding the word whose meaning is MOST NEARLY the same as that of the capitalized word.

33. AEROSOL, a _____ dispersed in a _____

    A. gas; liquid
    B. liquid; gas
    C. liquid; solid
    D. solid; liquid

34. ETIOLOGY

    A. cause of a disease
    B. method of cure
    C. method of diagnosis
    D. study of insects

35. IN VITRO, in

    A. alkali
    B. the body
    C. the test tube
    D. vacuum

KEY (CORRECT ANSWERS)

1. C		16. A	
2. B		17. B	
3. C		18. C	
4. A		19. D	
5. A		20. B	
6. B		21. D	
7. D		22. B	
8. A		23. A	
9. D		24. C	
10. A		25. B	
11. D		26. D	
12. B		27. B	
13. A		28. C	
14. B		29. B	
15. A		30. D	

31. B
32. A
33. B
34. A
35. C

BRIEF GLOSSARY OF STATISTICAL TERMS

		Page
I.	DESCRIPTIVE STATISTICS	1
	A. Frequency distribution	1
	B. Measures of the average or the central tendency	1
	1. The mean	1
	2. The median	1
	3. The mode	1
	C. Measures of variation	1
	1. The range	1
	2. The standard deviation or Sigma	1
	3. The variance	2
	D. Measures of Correlation	2
	1. The Pearson Product-Moment Correlation Coefficient	2
	2. The ranked correlation coefficient	2
II.	INFERENTIAL STATISTICS	2
	A. Principal measures of statistical significance	2
	1. Chi square	3
	2. Critical ratio	3
	3. t-test	3
	4. F-test	3
	5. Analysis of Variance	3

BRIEF GLOSSARY OF STATISTICAL TERMS

I. DESCRIPTIVE STATISTICS (Descriptive statistics simply summarize in numerical terms the characteristics of a set of data. Such characteristics include measures of central tendency, spread, correlation, and the like.)

   A. Frequency distribution

      This is a tabulation, sometimes presented in graphical form, showing the frequencies of the value of the variable when these values are arranged in order of magnitude. The frequency distribution is typically the first step in analyzing a set of data.

   B. Measures of the average or the central tendency

      The three MOST common indices are the mean, the median, and the mode.

      1. The mean is the arithmetic average, usually designated as M or X. It is computed by summing X all the scores and dividing by the number of measurements in the set.
      2. The median is the middle value in a set of scores that is, the point on the scale of the frequency distribution below and above which exactly 50% of the observation occur.
      3. The mode is the most common value in a frequency distribution. It is therefore possible for a distribution to have more than one mode.

Of the three measures listed above, the mean is the MOST commonly used, since it lends itself most readily to treatment by inferential statistics. The median has the advantage of being much easier to compute when the number of cases is 50 or less, and is also less influenced by extreme values. The mode is the MOST easily determined of the three, since it can usually be seen through directed inspection of the frequency distribution. The PRINCIPLE disadvantage of the mode is the difficulties it presents for inferential analysis.

   C. Measures of variation

      Summary description of the frequency distribution requires not only identification of the central tendency but some indication of the extent of spread of dispersion about this central value. Measures of the variation are used for this purpose.

      1. The range is the simplest measure of dispersion. It is simply the difference between the smallest and largest measurement in the series. Like the mode, the range is readily determined, but does not lend itself to statistical treatment.
      2. The standard deviation or Sigma (symbolized by SD or Z) is the MOST important, frequently used measure of dispersion. Algebraically, the standard deviation is obtained by expressing each measure as a deviation from the mean, squaring this deviation, summing all the squares, dividing by the number of observations, and taking the square root of this last value. In short, the standard deviation is the root mean square. The standard deviation may be used to compare the relative spread of two or more distributions. The standard deviation also serves as the basis for transforming distributions based on quite different units to the same scale. This is accomplished by expressing each measurement as a deviation from its mean and then dividing this by

the standard deviation to yield what is called a standard score or z-score. For example, in standard tests of achievement, scores in different subject matters are made comparable by transforming them into standard scores.
3. The variance is the square of the standard deviation. It is seldom used as a measure of dispersion all by itself, but it is important as the basis for inferential statistics which have to take into account the amount of dispersion in the data (see analysis of variance below).

D. Measures of Correlation

Measures of correlation or association describe the extent to which one variable is related to another.

1. The MOST common measure of association is the Pearson Product-Moment Correlation Coefficient designated by r. Perfect correspondence between two variables is expressed by an r of 1.00; perfect inverse correspondence (i.e., as one increases the other decreases) is expressed by an r of 1.00; complete lack of correspondence is reflected by an r of 0.00. The correlation coefficient should not be interpreted as a per cent. For example, the fact that the correlation between height and weight is approximately .80 does not mean that one can predict height from weight correctly 80% of the time. Whether a correlation is to be regarded as high or low depends on the variables involved and the question being asked. For example, a correlation of .60 between an intelligence test administered in grade school and subsequent performance in college would be regarded as spectacularly high. The same correlation betwen two forms of an individual intelligence test such as the Stanford-Binet would be unacceptably low. The last example illustrates a common application of the correlation coefficient as an index of reliability; that is, the extent to which the same or presumably equivalent measurement procedures yield similar results.
2. The ranked correlation coefficient is a measure of association based on ranks rather than raw scores. It also ranges from -1.00 to +1.00. It is much easier to compute an r when the number of cases is relatively small, but it is not quite as reliable.

II. INFERENTIAL STATISTICS (Inferential statistics go one step further and measure the extent to which a descriptive statistic based on a particular sample may be regarded as an estimate of characteristics of the larger universe from which the sample is drawn. Examples of inferential statistics include all tests of statistical significance.)

A. The MOST common use of inferential statistics is to determine the extent to which a result based on a particular sample can be regarded as an accurate estimate of the state of affairs in the total universe from which the sample is drawn. In other words, inferential statistics are used to determine the extent to which an obtained result might vary from the true one as a function of chance. Such inferential statistics are called tests of statistical significance and are evaluated in terms of the probability level (P) that the obtained result could have occurred by chance. These levels of probability, also called confidence limits, are set arbitrarily usually at either the 1% or 5% level; that is, the level at which the obtained result would be obtained by chance either one or five times out of a hundred. The PRINCIPAL measures of statistical significance are as follows:

1. Chi square (X^2)

   When the obtained results take the form of frequencies, proportions, or percentages rather than scores, the most common index for measuring the statistical significance of differences in such ration is X^2. The value of X^2 at the 5% and 1% level varies with the number of categories or cells being compared and the number of cases in each cell. Accordingly, to evaluate a particular X2 value it is necessary to consult a table to be found in virtually every elementary statistical text.

2. Critical ratio (CR)

   This index is used to test the statistical difference between two means when the number of cases in each group is large. The critical ratio is nowadays being supplanted by the t-test (see below) which takes into account the number of cases in each comparison.

3. t-test

   This is the MOST common and MOST efficient measure of the statistical difference between two means. It is a ratio which again varies depending on sample size so that significant levels must be determined from appropriate tables appearing in elementary statistical texts.

4. F-test

   This is a more general case of the t-test, used for comparing not just two but any number of means. In the simple case where only two means are involved F equals t . The F-test is the basic index employed for analysis of variance (see below).

5. Analysis of Variance

   A type of experimental design that permits the testing of significant differences across several different dimensions at once. For example, in an investigation involving not only an experimental group and a control group but subjects of both sexes classified in four different socio-economic classes, it is possible through the use of a balanced design to apply analysis of variance to determine significant differences that may exist not only between the experimenta.1 and control groups, but also between sexes, and SES levels, as well as their various combinations. The analysis of variance makes use of F-tests to determine whether obtained results achieve required levels of confidence.

GLOSSARY OF MEDICAL TERMS

CONTENTS

		Page
Abduction	Arteriosclerosis	1
Artery	Biceps Muscle	2
Bifida	Causalgia	3
Cullulitis	Colon	4
Comminuted	Dermaphytosis	5
Desiccation	Dysuria	6
Ecchymosis	Epigastric	7
Epilepsy, Jacksonian	Fascia	8
Felon	Genito-Urinary	9
Genu	Herniotomy	10
Humerus	Intertrochanteric	11
Intervertebral	Leucocytosis	12
Leucopenia	Metabolism	13
Metacarpus	Neuroma	14
Neuropsychiatric	Orthopnea	15
Os	Paraplegia	16
Paravertebral	Periosteum	17
Periphery	Pneumonia	18
Pneumonoconiosis	Pyelogram	19
Pyogenic	Scaphoid	20
Scapula	Supinate	21
Suture	Tibia	22
Tinnitus	Ununited	23
Ureter	Zygoma	24

GLOSSARY OF MEDICAL TERMS

A

Abduction
Movement of limb away from middle line of the body.
Abrasion
A scraping away of a portion of the skin.
Abscess
Localized collection of pus or matter.
Acetabulum
Cup-shaped depression on external surface of the pelvic bone (innominate) into which the head of femur, or thighbone, fits.
Achilles Reflex
Movement of foot downward when the tendon immediately above the heel bone is struck.
Acromion
Process of bone constituting tip of shoulder.
Adduction
Movement of limb toward middle line of body.
Adhesion
The matting together of two surfaces by inflammation.
Alae Nash
Outer flaring walls of the nostrils.
Allergic
Reaction of tissues of the body to a protein substance to which the body is especially sensitive.
Anemia
A condition in which the red blood cells and/or hemoglobin are reduced.
Aneurysm
Sac, filled with blood, formed by the local dilation of walls of artery.
Angina Pectoris
Pain in chest associated with heart disease.
Ankyloses
Complete absence of motion at a joint.
Anterior
The anatomical "front" of the body.
Aorta
Main trunk of the systemic arterial system, arising from base of left ventricle.
Apex
Extremity of conical or pyramidal structure, such as heart or lung.
Aphasia
Loss of power of speech by damage to speech center.
Apoplexy
Another word for stroke.
Arrhythmia
Loss of normal rhythm of the heart.
Arteriosclerosis
Hardening of the arteries.

Artery
Blood vessel conveying blood away from the heart to different parts of the body.
Arthritis
Inflammation of a joint.
Arthrodesis
Stiffening of a joint.
Articulation
Joint.
Asbestosis
Dust disease of asbestos workers.
Aseptic
Free of germs.
Aspiration
Withdrawal, by suction, of air or fluid from any cavity.
Asthma
Disease marked by recurrent attacks of shortness, of breath, due to temporary change in bronchial tubes, making person uncomfortable.
Astigmatism
An abnormality in the curve of the 'anterior visual surface of the eyeball.
Astragalus
One of the ankle bones.
Ataxia
Disturbance of coordination of muscular movements.
Atelectasis
Collapse of lung tissue due to failure of entrance of air into air-cells.
Atrophy
Wasting or diminution in size of a structure.
Audiogram
Graphic record made by an audiometer, an electrical instrument for recording acuity of hearing.
Auricular fibrillation
Irregular beat as to time and force beginning in auricle of the heart.
Auscultation
The act of listening to sounds within the body.
Axillary
Relating to armpit.

B

Baker's Cyst
Enlargement of synovial sac in the back of the knee joint.
Basal Metabolism
The energy expended for the absolute minimum requirements of the body at complete rest.
Bell's Palsy
A form of facial paralysis.
Benign
Not malignant.
Biceps Muscle
A muscle over front of arm.

Bifida
   Split or cleft.
Bilateral
   Relating to or having two sides.
Blood Pressure
   Pressure or tension of the blood within the arteries.
Brachial
   Pertaining to the arm.
Bradycardia
   Abnormal slowness of the heartbeat.
Brain
   Mass of nerve tissue which is contained within the skull.
Bronchiectasis
   Dilation of the narrowest portions of the breathing tubes of the lung.
Bronchitis
   Inflammation of mucus membrane of bronchial tubes.
Buerger's Disease
   Thromboangiitis obliterans; obliteration and inflammation of the larger arteries and veins of a limb by clotting and inflammation, involving nerve trunks.
Bursa
   A lubricating sac usually found at pressure points or around joints.
Bursitis
   Inflammation of the bursa.

C

Calcaneum
   The os calcis, or heel bone.
Calcification
   X-ray opaque substance found in serious tissues of the body.
Canthus
   Either extremity of the slit between the eyelids.
Capitellum
   Portion of bone found at the end of the arm bone.
Capsule
   Fibrous membrane which envelopes an organ, joint or a foreign body.
Carbuncle
   Group of boils resulting in localized gangrene or death of affected tissues.
Cardiac
   Pertaining to the heart.
Cardiologist
   Heart specialist.
Catheter
   Hollow cylinder of silver, India rubber or other material, designed to be passed into a hollow area for drainage purposes.
Cartilage
   White substance which covers ends of bones.
Causalgia
   A painful condition.

Cellulitis
　　Diffuse inflammation of cellular tissue, i.e., especially loose cellular tissue just underneath skin.
Cephalalgia
　　Headache.
Cerebellum
　　Back part of the brain, concerned in coordination of movements.
Cerebrum
　　Front part of the brain, concerned with the conscious processes of the mind.
Cervix
　　Neck or neck-like part.
Charcot's joint
　　Painless joint destruction.
Cholecystectomy
　　Surgical removal of the gall-bladder.
Cholecystis
　　Inflammation of gall-bladder.
Cholelithiasis
　　Gallstone.
Chorio-Retinal
　　Relating to the visual tissue of eye and its supporting structure.
Chondral
　　Pertaining to cartilage.
Cicatrix
　　Scar.
Cirrhosis
　　Fibrosis or sclerosis of any organ; hardening.
Clavicle
　　Collar bone.
Clonus
　　Muscular spasm in which contraction and relaxation of muscle follow one another in rapid succession.
Coccydynia
　　Pain in the coccyx.
Coccygectomy
　　Removal of the coccyx.
Coccygeal
　　Relating to the coccyx.
Coccyx
　　Small bone at the end of the spinal column in man.
Congenital
　　Existing at birth.
Congestion
　　Engorgement of blood vessels of a part.
Conjunctiva
　　Delicate membrane which lines the inner surface of the eyelids and covers the eyeball in front.
Colles Fracture
　　Fracture of lower end of radius
Colon
　　The last part of the intestinal tract.

Comminuted
   Broken into more than two fragments.
Concussion
   Injury of a soft structure, as the brain, resulting from a blow or violent shaking.
Coronary Artery
   The artery providing nutrition to the heart muscle.
Cornea
   Transparent structure forming the anterior part of the external layer of eyeball.
Cortex
   Outer portion of an organ, such as the kidney, as distinguished from inner or medullary portion; external layer of gray matter covering hemispheres of cerebrum and cerebellum.
Costal
   Pertaining to the ribs.
Coxa
   Hip joint.
Cranium
   Skull.
Crepitus
   Abnormal sounds heard in the case of fractured bones and diseased tissues when rubbing together.
Curettage
   Scraping the interior of a cavity for the removal of tissue.
Cutaneous
   Relating to the skin.
Cyanosis
   Blueish discoloration of external tissue, e.g. lips, nails, skin.
Cyst
   Abnormal sac which contains a liquid or semi-solid.
Cystoscopy
   Inspection of the interior of the bladder with a cystoscope.
Cystostomy
   Formation of a more or less permanent opening into the urinary bladder.

D

Dactyl
   Digit: Finger or toe.
Decompensation
   Failure to maintain normal function as in heart failure.
Deltoid
   Triangular-shaped muscle of the shoulder.
Dementia
   Form of insanity.
Dermatitis
   Inflammation of the skin.
Dermatologist
   Skin specialist.
Dermaphytosis
   Skin disease due to presence of a vegetable microparasite.

Desiccation
The removal of tissue by chemical, physical, electrical, freezing, or x-ray.
Diabetes (Melitus)
A disease having symptoms of excessive urine and sugar excretion.
Diaphragm
Muscular partition between thorax and abdomen.
Diarrhea
Abnormally frequent discharge of fluid fecal matter from the bowel.
Diastasis
Simple separation of normally joined parts.
Diastole
Period of rest during which heart is filling up for next beat.
Diathermy
Local elevation of temperature in tissues, produced by special form of high-frequency current.
Diathesis
Predisposition to a disease.
Digit
Finger or toe.
Dilatation
Enlargement, due to stretching or thinning out of tissues.
Diplopia
Double-vision.
Disc
A round flat surface variously found in eye and spinal column conditions.
Dislocation
Most frequently used in orthopedics to describe a disturbance of normal relationship of bones which enter into formation of a joint.
Distal
Farthest from the point of origin; the term is usually used in connection with the extremities.
Diverticulum
Pouch or sac opening out from a tubular organ.
Dorsal
Relating to the back; posterior.
Dorsum
The back; upper or posterior surface or back of any part.
Duct
Tube or passage with well-defined walls for passing excretions or secretions.
Duodenum
Upper portion of intestinal tube connecting with stomach.
Dupuytren's Contraction
Contraction of the palmar fascia causing permanent flexion of one or more fingers.
Dura Mater
Outermost and toughest of three membranes covering brain and spinal cord.
Dysphagia
Difficulty in swallowing.
Dyspnoea
Difficulty in breathing.
Dysuria
Difficulty or pain in urination.

E

Ecchymosis
　　Black and blue spot on the skin.
Ectropion
　　A rolling outward of the margin of an eyelid.
Eczema
　　A form of dermatitis.
Edema
　　Swelling due to watery effusion in the intercellular spaces.
Electrocardiogram
　　Graph of electric currents in the heart.
Electrocardiograph
　　Instrument for producing electrocardiogram.
Embolus
　　Clot or plug brought by blood-current from distant part.
Embolism
　　The plugging up of a blood vessel by a floating mass.
Eminence
　　Circumscribed area raised above general area of surrounding surface.
Emphysema
　　Abnormal distention with loss of elasticity of the air sacs of the lung.
Empyema
　　Accumulation of pus or matter in normally closed cavity on the surface of the lung.
Encephalitis
　　Inflammation of the brain substance.
Encephalogram
　　Roentgenogram of contents of the skull.
Encephalopathy
　　Conditions of disease of the brain.
Endocrine Gland
　　A gland which furnishes internal secretion.
Endogenous
　　Originating or produced within organism or one of its parts.
Enophthalmos
　　Recession of the eyeball within the orbit.
Epicardium
　　Cover of the heart.
Epicondyle
　　Projection from long bone near articular extremity above or upon condyle.
Epidermis
　　Outermost layer of the skin.
Epididymis
　　Oblong or boat-shaped body located on back of testicle.
Epidural
　　Upon the outer envelope of the brain.
Epigastric
　　Depression at pit of abdominal wall at tip of sword-shaped cartilage of sternum.

Epilepsy, Jacksonian
Convulsive contractions affecting localized groups of muscles without disturbance of mentality.
Epiphysis
Ends of long bones.
Epistaxis
Bloody nose.
Epithelium
Covering of skin and mucus membrane consisting of epithelial cells.
Epithelioma
Cancer of the skin or mucus membrane.
Erector spinae
Muscle keeping the spine erects.
Eruption
A breaking out; redness, spotting or other visible phenomena on the skin or mucus membrane.
Erythema
Abnormal redness of the skin.
Esophagus
Gullet. Tube connecting mouth to stomach.
Etiology
Cause.
Eversion
A turning outward, as of the eyelid or foot.
Exacerbation
Increase in severity of disease or symptoms.
Excision
Operative removal of a portion of an organ.
Excrescence
Outgrowth from the surface, especially a pathological growth.
Exogenous
Originating or produced outside.
Exophthalmus
Protrusion or prominence of the eyeball.
Exostosis
Bony tumor springing from surface of a bone, most commonly seen at muscular attachments.
Extensor
A muscle the contraction of which tends to straighten a limb.
Extrasystole
Premature contraction of one or more heart chambers.
Exudate
A fluid, often coagulable, extravasated into tissue or cavity.

F

Facies
Face, countenance, expression; surface.
Fascia
Sheet or band of fibrous tissue.

Felon
   Abscess in terminal phalanx of a finger.
Femoral
   Relating to the femur or thigh.
Femur
   Thigh bone.
Fibrillation
   Totally irregular beat.
Fibroma
   Fibroid tumor.
Fibrosis
   Pathological formation of fibrous tissue.
Fibula
   Smaller calf bone.
Fistula
   Abnormal passageway leading to surface of body.
Flexion
   Bending of a joint.
Flexor
   A muscle the action of which is to flex a joint.
Follicle
   Very small excretory or secretory sac or gland.
Foramen
   Aperture through a bone or membranous structure.
Fracture, Comminuted
   Bone broken into more than two pieces.
Fracture, Ununited
   One in which union fails to occur.
Frontal
   Relating to the front of body.
Fundus
   Base of a hollow organ.
Fusiform
   Spindle-shaped, tapering at both ends.

G

Ganglion
   Usually used to describe a cystic tumor occurring on a tendon sheath or in connection with a joint.
Gangrene
   Death or masse of any part of the body.
Gastric
   Pertaining to the stomach.
Gastrocnemius
   One of the calf muscles.
Genitalia
   Organs of reproduction.
Genito-Urinary
   Relation to reproduction and urination, noting organs concerned.

Genu
    Knee.
Genu-Valgum
    Knock-knee.
Gladiolus
    Middle and largest division of sternum (chest bone).
Gland
    Secreting organ.
Glaucoma
    Increased pressure in the eyeball.
Gluteal
    Pertaining to the buttocks.
Greenstick Fracture
    Incomplete fracture.
Gynecologist
    Specialist in the treatment of diseases peculiar to women.

H

Hallux
    Great toe.
Hallux valgus
    Deviation of great toe toward inner or lateral side of the foot (bunion).
Haematemesis
    Vomiting of blood.
Haemoglobin
    Coloring matter of blood in red blood corpuscles.
Haemoptysis
    Discharge of blood from the lungs by coughing.
Hemarthrosis
    Effusion of blood into cavity of a joint.
Hematoma
    Swelling formed by effused blood.
Hematuria
    Passage of blood in the urine.
Hemianopsia
    Loss of vision for one-half of visual field.
Hemorrhage
    Bleeding, especially if profuse.
Hemorrhoids
    Piles, a varicose condition causing painful swellings of the anus.
Hepatic
    Pertaining to the liver.
Herania
    Protrusion of organ outside of its normal confines.
Hernioplasty
    Operation for hernia.
Herniotomy
    Operation for relief of hernia.

Humerus
   Bone of the upper arm.
Hydrarthrosis
   Effusion of a serous fluid into a joint cavity.
Hydrocele
   Circumscribed collection of fluid around the testicle.
Hydrone Phrosis
   Dilatation inside kidney due to obstruction of flow of urine.
Hyperaesthesia
   Excessive sensitiveness of the skin to touch or hypersensitiveness of any special sense.
Hyperglycaemia
   Abnormally large proportion of sugar in blood.
Hypertension
   High blood pressure often associated with arteriosclerosis.
Hyperthrophy
   Enlargement, general increase in bulk of a part or organ, not due to tumor formation.
Hypogastrium
   Lower middle region of the abdomen.
Hypoplasia
   Under-development of structure.
Hypothenar
   Fleshy mass at the inner (little finger) side of the palm.
Hysteria
   A functional nervous condition characterized by lack of emotional control and sudden temporary attacks of mental, emotional or physical aberration.

I

Ileum
   Portion of the small intestine.
Ilium
   One of the bones of the pelvis.
Impacted
   Driven in firmly.
Incontinence
   Inability to retain a natural discharge.
Induration
   Hardening; spot or area of hardened tissue
Infarct
   Death of tissue due to lack of blood supply
Inguinal
   Relating to the groin.
In situ
   In position.
Intercostal
   Between the ribs
Interstitial
   Relating to spaces within any structure.
Intertrochanteric
   Between the two trochanters of the femur or thigh bone

Intervertebral
    Between two vertebrae.
Iris
    Circular colored portion of the eye which surrounds pupil
Ischaemia
    Local and temporary deficiency of blood.
Ischium
    One of the pelvic bones.

J

Jaundice
    Yellowness of tissues due to absorption of bile.
Jejunum
    Portion of small intestine about 8 feet long, between duodenum and ileum.

K

Kienboeck Disease
    Increased porosity and softness of certain carpal bones.
Keloid
    Peculiar overgrowth of hyaline connective tissues in the skin of predisposed individuals after injury or scarring.
Keratitis
    Inflammation of the cornea.
Kyphosis
    Curvature of the spine, hump-back, hunch-back.

L

Laceration
    Separation of tissue (cut).
Lacriminal
    Relating to the tears apparatus.
Laminae
    Flattened portions of the sides of a vertebral arch.
Laminectomy
    Removal of one or more laminae from the vertebrae.
Larynx
    Organ of voice production.
Lesion
    Any hurt, wound or degeneration.
Leucocytosis
    Temporary increase in relative number of white blood cells in the blood.

Leucopenia
　　Abnormal decrease in number of white blood corpuscles.
Ligament
　　Tough fibrous band which connects one bone with another.
Lipoma
　　Tumor composed of fatty tissue.
Lordosis
　　Anteroposterior curvature of the spine (opposite to kyphosis).
Lue tic
　　Syphilitic.
Lumbar
　　Lower back.
Lumbar Vertebrae
　　The five vertebrae between the thoracic vertebrae and the sacrum.
Luxation
　　Dislocation.
Lymphangitis
　　Inflammation of the lymphatic vessels.

M

Malar
　　Relating to the cheek-bone.
Malignant
　　Resistant to treatment; occurring in severe form; tending to grow worse and (in the case of a tumor) to recur after removal. Usually indicates poor end result.
Malleoli
　　Rounded bony prominences on both sides of the ankle joint.
Mandible
　　Lower jaw.
Manubrium
　　Upper portion of the sternum.
Mastectomy
　　Amputation of the breast.
Maxilla
　　Upper jaw.
Meatus
　　Passage or opening.
Meninges
　　Membranes, specifically the envelope of brain and spinal cord.
Meningitis
　　Inflammation of the meninges.
Meniscus
　　Intraarticular fibrocartilage of crescentic or discoid shape found in certain joints.
Mesentery
　　Web or membrane connecting bowel tube to posterior abdominal wall (a portion of the peritoneum).
Metabolism
　　The total operation of building up and breaking down tissues.

Metacarpus
Part of hand between wrist and fingers; palm; five metacarpal bones collectively which form skeleton of this part.
Metastasis
Transfer of disease, usually malignant, to remote part of the body.
Metatarsalgia
Pain in the region of the metatarsus(or ball of foot).
Metatarsus
Anterior portion of foot between instep and toes, having as its skeleton five long bones articulating anteriorly with the phalanges.
Mottling
Spotting with patches of varying shades of colors.
Mucocutaneous
Relating to mucus membrane and skin, noting the line of junction of the two at the nasal, oral, vaginal and anal orifices.
Musculature
Arrangement of muscles in a part or in the body as a whole.
Myalgia
Muscular pain.
Myelitis
Inflammation of the substance of the spinal cord.
Myelograph
X-ray picture of spinal cord using radio-opaque substance.
Myocardium
Heart Muscle.
Myocarditis
Inflammation of the muscular walls of the heart.
Myositis
Inflammation of a muscle.

N

Navicular
Boat-shaped, noting a bone in the wrist and one in the ankle.
Nausea
Sickness at the stomach; inclination to vomit.
Nephritis
Inflammation of the kidney.
Necrosis
Death en masse of a portion of tissue.
Nephrosis
Non-inflammatory disease of the kidney.
Neuralgia
Pain radiating along a nerve.
Neuritis
Inflammation of a nerve.
Neurologist
Nerve specialist.
Neuroma
Tumor made up largely of nerve tissue.

Neuropsychiatric
Relating to disease of both mind and nervous system.
Neurosis
Functional derangement of the nervous system.
Nocturia
Bed-wetting.
Node
Knob; circumscribed swelling; circumscribed mass of differentiated tissue; knuckle.
Nucleus Pulposus
Gelatinous center of an intervertebral disc.
Nystagmus
Continuous movement of the eyeballs in the horizontal or vertical plains.

O

Occipital
Relating to the back of the head.
Occlude
To close up or fit together.
Occular
Relating to the eye; visual.
Occult
Hidden; concealed, noting a concealed hemorrhage, the blood being so changed as not to be readily recognized.
Olecranon
Tip of the elbow.
Omentum
Web or apron-like membranous structure lying in front of the intestines.
Opacities
Areas lacking in transparency.
Opthalmia
Disease of the eye.
Opthalmologist
Specialist in eye diseases and refractive errors of the eye.
Optic
Relating to the eye or to vision.
Optometrist
Person without medical training who fits glasses to correct visual defects.
Orbit
Eye- socket.
Orchitis
Inflammation of the testicle.
Orchidectomy
Castration; removal of one or both testicles.
Orthopedics
Branch of surgery which has to do with treatment of diseases of joints and spine and correction of deformities.
Orthopnea
Ability to breathe with comfort only when sitting erect or standing.

Os
    Bone
Oscalcis
    Heel-bone.
Ossification
    Formation of bone; change into bone.
Osteoma
    Bone tumor.
Osteomyelitis
    Inflammation of bone and bone marrow.
Osteoporosis
    Disease of bone marked by increased porosity and softness ("thinning" of bone).
Osteotomy
    Cutting a bone, usually by saw or chisel, for removal of a piece of dead bone, correction of knock-knee or other deformity, or for any purpose whatsoever.
Otologist
    Specialist in diseases of the ear.

P

Paget's Disease
    Usually refers to a bone disease.
Pancreas
    Abdominal digestive gland, extending from duodenum to spleen, containing insulin forming cells.
Palate
    Roof of the mouth.
Palliative
    Mitigating; reducing in severity, noting a method of treating a disease or its symptoms.
Palmar
    Referring to the palm of the hand.
Palpate
    To examine by feeling and pressing with the palms and fingers.
Palpebral
    Relating to an, eyelid or the eyelids.
Papule
    Pimple.
Palsy
    Paralysis.
Paraesthesia
    Abnormal spontaneous sensation, such as a burning, pricking, numbness.
Paralysis
    Loss of power of motion.
Paralysis Agitans
    Shaking paralysis, Parkinson's Disease.
Paraplegia
    Paralysis of legs and lower parts of the body.

Paravertebral
　　Alongside a vertebra or the spinal column.
Parenchymal
　　Relating to the specific tissue of a gland or organ.
Paresis
　　Incomplete paralysis.
Parietal
　　Pertaining to the walls.
Parkinson's Syndrome
　　Aggregate symptoms, including raised eyebrows and expressionless face, of paralysis agitans.
Paronychia
　　Inflammation of structures surrounding the nail or the bone itself of finger or toe.
Paralysis Agitans
　　Shaking paralysis, Parkinson's Disease.
Paraplegia
　　Paralysis of legs and lower parts of the body.
Paravertebral
　　Alongside a vertebra or the spinal column.
Parenchymal
　　Relating to the specific tissue of a gland or organ.
Paresis
　　Incomplete paralysis.
Parietal
　　Pertaining to the walls.
Parkinson's Syndrome
　　Aggregate symptoms, including raised eyebrows and expressionless face, of paralysis agitans.
Paronychia
　　Inflammation of structures surrounding the nail or the bone itself of finger or toe.
Passive
　　Not active.
Past-Pointing
　　Test of integrity of vestibular apparatus of the ear by rotating person in revolving chair.
Patella
　　Knee-cap.
Pathology
　　Branch of medicine which treats of the abnormal tissues in disease.
Pectoral
　　Relating to the chest.
Pedicle
　　Stalk or stem forming the attachment of a tumor which is non-sessile, i.e., which does not have a broad base of attachment.
Pellegrini, Stieda's Disease
　　Bony growth over the internal condyle of the femur, a sequel of stieda's fracture.
Pendulous
　　Hanging freely or loosely.
Pericardium
　　Sac enveloping the heart.
Periosteum
　　Thick, fibrous membrane covering the entire surface of a bone.

Periphery
>Outer part or surface.

Peristalsis
>Worm-like movement of the gastro-intestinal tract.

Peritoneum
>Serous membrane which covers abdominal organs and inner aspect of abdominal walls.

Peritonitis
>Inflammation of the peritoneum.

Peroneal
>Pertaining to the outer aspects of the leg.

Pes
>Foot; foot-like or basal structure or part.

Pes Cavus
>Exaggeration of the normal arch of the foot; hollowfoot.

Pes Equinus
>Permanent extension of the foot so that only the ball rests on the ground.

Petechial
>Relating to minute hemorrhagic spots, of pinpoint to pinhead size, in the skin.

Phalanx
>Bone of a finger or toe.

Phlebitis
>Inflammation of the veins.

Physiology
>Science which treats of functions of different parts of the body.

Physiotherapy
>Use of natural forces in the treatment of disease, as in electro-hydro, and aero-therapy, massage, and therapeutic exercises, and use of mechanical devices in mechanotherapy.

Pill-RollingTremor
>Tremor in paralysis agitans in the form of circular movement of opposed tips of thumb and index finger.

Pilonidal Cyst
>Cyst at the lower end of the spine.

Pisiform
>Pea-shaped or pea-sized.

Plantar
>Relating to the sole of the foot.

Pleura
>Serous membrane which invests lungs and covers inner part of the chest walls (similar to peritoneum in abdominal cavity.)

Pleurisy
>Inflammation of the pleura.

Plexus
>Network or tangle of nerves.

Plumbism
>Lead poisoning.

Pneumoconiosis
>Dust disease of the lungs.

Pneumonia
>Inflammation of lung substance.

Pneumonoconiosis
   Fibrous hardening of the lungs due to irritation caused by inhalation of dust incident to various occupations.

Pneumothorax
   Presence of air or gas in the pleural cavity.

Poliomyelitis
   Inflammation of the anterior portion of the spinal cord.

Polyp
   Pedunculated swelling or outgrowth from a mucus membrane.

Polyuria
   Excessive excretion of urine.

Popliteal
   Relating to the posterior surface of the knee.

Precordium
   Anterior surface of lower part of the thorax.

Pretibial
   Relating to anterior portion of the leg.

Proliferative
   Excess growth.

Pronate
   To rotate the forearm in such a way that the palm of the hand looks backward when the arm is in the anatomical position, or downward when the arm is extended at a right angle with the body.

Prostate
   Gland surrounding neck of the male bladder.

Prostatectomy
   Removal of all or part of the prostate.

Protuberance
   Outgrowth: swelling; knob.

Proximal
   Nearest the trunk or point of origin, said of part of an extremity, artery or nerve so situated.

Psychiatrist
   Alienist; one who specializes in diseases of the mind.

Psychogenic
   Of mental origin or causation.

Ptosis
   Drooping down of an eyelid or an organ.

Pubic
   One of the bones of the pelvis.

Pulmonic
   Relating to the lungs.

Puritis
   Itching irritation.

Purulent
   Having the appearance of pus or matter.

Pyelitis
   Inflammation of a portion of the kidney.

Pyelogram
   Roentgenogram of the area of the kidneys and ureter, by use of opaque substances.

Pyogenic
   Pus-forming.

R

Radiologist
   One skilled in the diagnostic and therapeutic use of x-rays.
Radius
   Outer and shorter of the two bones of forearm.
Rales
   Sounds of varied character heard on auscultation of the chest in cases of disease of the lungs or bronchi.
Rectum
   Terminal portion of the digestive tube.
Reflex
   Involuntary or reflected action or movement.
Renal
   Pertaining to the kidney.
Resection
   Removal of articular ends of one or both bones forming a joint, or of a segment of any part, such as the intestine.
Respiration
   Function common to all living plants or animals, consisting in taking in of oxygen and throwing off products of oxidation in the tissues, mainly carbon dioxide and water.
Retina
   Inner, nervous tunic of the eyeball, consisting of an outer pigment layer and an inner layer formed by expansion of the optic nerve.
Retrosternal
   Behind the sternum.
Rib
   One of twenty-four elongated curved bones forming the main portion of bony wall of the chest.
Rhinitis
   Inflammation of the nasal mucus membrane.
Roentgenologist
   One skilled in the diagnostic and therapeutic use of x-rays.

S

Sacroiliac
   Relating to sacrum and ilium, noting articulation between the two bones and associated ligaments.
Sacrum
   Triangular bone at the base of the spine.
Sarcoma
   Malignant tumor of fibrous tissue or its derivatives.
Scaphoid
   Boat-shaped; hollowed.

Scapula
   Shoulder-blade.
Sciatica
   Painful affection of the sciatic nerve.
Sclerosis
   Hardness
Scoliosis
   Lateral curvature of the spine.
Scrotum
   Sac containing testes.
Semilunar Cartilages
   Two intraarticular fibrocartilages of the knee-joint.
Senile
   Relating to or characteristic of old age.
Septicemia
   Morbid condition due to presence of septic microbes and their poisons in the blood.
Sequela
   Morbid condition following as a consequence of another disease.
Sesamoid.
   Resembling in size or shape a grain of sesame.
Sequestrum
   Piece of dead bone separated from living bone.
Shock
   Sudden vital depression due to injury or emotion which makes an untoward depression.
Siderosis
   Form of dust disease due to presence of iron dust.
Silicosis
   Form of dust disease due to inhalation of stone dust.
Sinusitis
   Inflammation of the lining membrane of any sinus, especially of one of the accessory sinuses of the nose.
Spasm
   Sudden violent involuntary rigid contraction, due to muscular action.
Sphincter
   Orbicular muscle which, when in state of normal contraction, closes one of the orifices of the body.
Spina Bifida
   Limited defect in the spinal column consisting in absence of vertebral arches, through which defect spinal membranes protrude.
Spondylolisthesis
   Forward subluxation of body of vertebra on vertebra below it or on sacrum.
Sprain
   Wrenching of a joint.
Stenosis
   Narrowing of an orifice.
Sternoclavicular
   Relating to sternum and clavicle, noting an articulation and occasional muscle.
Stricture
   Abnormal narrowing of a channel.
Supinate
   To turn forearm and hand volar side uppermost.

Suture
Stitch.
Symphysis
Union between two bones by means of fibrocartilage.
Syncope
Fainting.
Syndrome
Complex of symptoms which occur together.
Synovitis
Inflammation of synovial membrane, especially of a joint.
Systole
Period of the heart-beat during which the heart is contracting.

T

Tachycardia
Abnormal increase in rate of the hearts beat, not subsiding on rest, sudden in onset and offset.
Tarsus
Root of the foot or instep.
Temporamandibular
Relating to the temporal bone (bone of the temple) and lower jaw, noting the articulation of the lower jaw.
Tendon
Inelastic fibrous cord or band in which muscle fibers ends and by which muscle is attached to bone or other structure.
Tendosynovitis
Inflammation of the sheath of a tendon.
Tetanus
Lockjaw.
Thorax
Chest, upper part of the trunk between neck and abdomen; it is formed by the twelve dorsal vertebrae, the twelve pairs of ribs, sternum, and muscles and fascias attached to these; it is separated from the abdomen by the diaphragm; it contains chief organs of circulatory and respiratory systems.
Thrombo Angitis Obliterans
Buerger's disease; obliteration of the larger arteries and veins of a limb by thrombi, with subsequent gangrene. See Buerger's Disease.
Thrombophlebitis
Thrombosis with inflammation of the veins.
Thrombosis
Formation of a clot of blood within a blood vessel.
Thyroid
Gland and cartilage of the larynx.
Thyroidectomy
Removal of the thyroid gland.
Tibia
Shin-bone; inner and larger of two bones of the leg.

Tinnitus
Subjective noises (ringing, whistling, booming, etc.) in the ears.
Tonsillitis
Inflammation of a tonsil.
Torticollis
Wry-neck; stiff-neck; spasmodic contraction of muscles of the neck; the head is drawn to one side and usually rotated so that the chin points the other side.
Torsion
Twisting or rotation of a part upon its axis; twisting the cut end of an artery to arrest hemmorhage.
Toxemia
Blood-poisoning.
Toxin
Poison.
Trachea
Windpipe.
Transillumination
Shining light through a translucent part to see if fluid is present.
Trapezius
Muscle extending from back of the head to shoulderbiade; it moves head and shoulder.
Trauma
Wound; injury inflicted usually more or less suddenly by physical agent.
Tremor
Trembling, shaking, loss of equilibrium.
Trephine
Cylindrical or crown saw used for removal of a disc of bone, especially from the skull, or of other firm tissue as that of the cornea.
Triceps
Three-headed muscle extending the forearm. (Covers posterior of upper arm).
Trochanter
One of two bony prominences developed from independent osseous centers near the upper extremity of the thigh bone.
Tubercle
Circumscribed, rounded, solid elevation on the skin, mucus membrane, or surface of an organ; lesion of tuberculosis consisting of a small isolated nodule or aggregation of nodules.
Tuberosity
Broad eminence of bone.

U

Ulcer
Open sore other than a wound.
Ulna
Inner and larger of the two bones of the forearm.
Umbilicus
Navel.
Ununited
Not united or knit, noting an unhealed fracture.

Ureter
    Musculomembranous tube leading from kidney to bladder.
Urethra
    Membranous tube leading from bladder to external exit.
Urination
    The passing of urine.
Urogram
    Roentgenogram of any part (kidneys, ureters, bladder) of the urinary tract, with the use of opaque substances.
Urologist
    One versed in the branch of medical science which has to do with urine and its modifications in disease.
Urtcaria
    Hives.
Uterus
    Womb.

V

Varicocele
    Varicose veins of the spermatic cord.
Varicose
    Dilated, as used in reference to veins.
Varix
    Enlarged and tortuous vein, artery, or lymphatic vessel.
Vas
    Vessel.
Vasomotor
    Regulating mechanism controlling expansion and contraction of blood vessels.
Ventral
    Relating to anterior portion.
Ventricular
    Relating to a ventricle.
Vertebra
    One of thirty-three bones of the spinal column.
Vertex
    Crown of the head; topmost point of the vault of the skull.
Vertigo
    Dizziness.
Vitiligo
    Appearance on the skin of white patches of greater or lesser extent, due to simple loss of pigment without other trophic changes.
Volar
    Referring to the palm of the hand.

Z

Zygoma
    Strong bar of bone bridging over the depression of the temple; cheek-bone.